THE CONFLICT of LAW AND JUSTICE in the ICELANDIC SAGAS

VALUE INQUIRY BOOK SERIES

VIBS

Volume 21

THE CONFLICT of LAW AND JUSTICE in the ICELANDIC SAGAS

William Pencak

Rodopi

Amsterdam - Atlanta, GA 1995

Cover design by Chris Kok based on a photograph, ©1984 by Robert Ginsberg, of statuary by Gustav Vigeland in the Frogner Park, Oslo, Norway.

♾ The paper on which this book is printed meets the requirements of "ISO 9706:1994, Information and documentation - Paper for documents - Requirements for permanence".

ISBN: 90-5183-835-2 (CIP)

Printed in The Netherlands

In Memory of My Grandparents:

Anna Pencak
Catherine Borgwardt
Max Borgwardt

TABLE OF CONTENTS

ICELAND

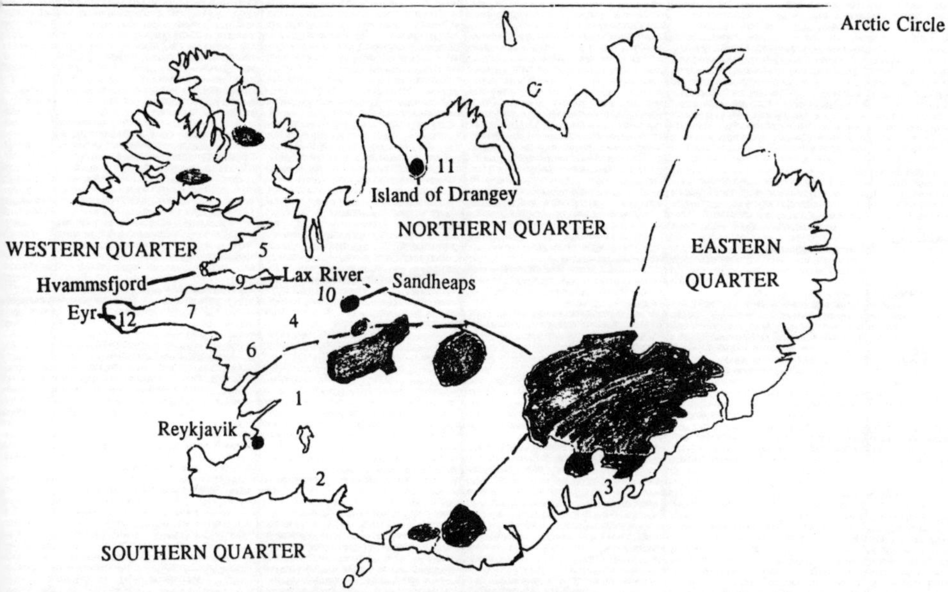

PRINCIPAL REGIONS OF SAGAS

1 - Thingvellir, site of Althing (*Bandamanna Saga* and "Ale-Hood")
2 - Site of *Njal's Saga*
3 - Svinafell
4 - Site of *Grettir's Saga*
5 - Site of *Laxdaela Saga*
6 - Site of *Egil's Saga*
7 - Site of *Eyrbyggja Saga*
8 - Hvammsfjord
9 - Lax River
10 - Sandheaps
11 - Island of Drangey
12 - Eyr

Notes:

Shaded areas represent glaciers.

\- - - - - - - - represent Quarter boundaries.

One inch (2.5 cm) equals approximately 60 miles or 100 kilometers.

LIST OF ILLUSTRATIONS

EDITORIAL FOREWORD

William Pencak has written a philosophical study of legal and political questions by examining their conflicts within a world-class body of related literature — the Icelandic sagas. While the sagas are celebrated for the exquisite poetry of their language and the dramatic power of their action, they might be most appealing to modern readers for the poignancy of their humanism. They movingly evoke the sufferings and faults of individual human beings caught up in the mess of social existence. We are caught up in the desires and adventures, the griefs and misadventures of these characters with whom we share identifiable traits. Pencak seizes upon the wealth of human relations that this material displays, tracing the ups and downs of individuals through the law system as that system falls apart. Frustration and collapse, aspiration and compromise are the recurrent themes.

Though the literature is centuries old and from an isolated country, the conflicts at stake are generally those that arise in liberal efforts at law and order. The struggles, heroism, and the tragedies in the sagas are related to the old Icelandic republic, yet in uncanny fashion they are of up-to-the minute interest. While the subject is literary, Pencak's treatment mostly deals with the issues raised rather than the literary merit: the problematic more than the plot.

Pencak has distinguished himself in his many scholarly contributions as historian, textual interpreter, semiotician, cultural analyst, philosophical thinker, and caring human being. A true multi-disciplinarian, he brings to the present volume a refreshingly original approach to traditional works and perduring problems. It has the rare merit of making a philosophical case study out of an historical crisis embedded in literary expression. The strained relationships between law, constitution, ethics, justice, power, and passion await your encounter as you accompany Pencak on his guided tour of the strangely familiar world of the Icelandic sagas.

Robert Ginsberg
Executive Editor

GUEST FOREWORD

I enjoy a three-fold pleasure in being able to write this prefatory note to Professor Pencak's lapidary monograph, *The Conflict of Law and Justice in the Icelandic Sagas:*

First, there is the pleasure and pride of collegiality and of friendship in seeing this latest work of Pencak join the world of intellectual, creative community.

Second, in Pencak's book I find a sharp focus on the Icelandic "Thing" as Court or place of judgment and assembly. Here we recognize the evolution of an idea of Thing. It begins as the designated place and space where conflicts of interest — indeed, of legal order and hence of types of discourse — confront one another and are resolved. It then develops into the modern notion of a "thing" as an actual entity and factive representation, such that "things" today are taken as shared evidence of a common world. This concept of the Thing in the Icelandic sagas, as Pencak writes, is both allusion and referent — textual and conceptual — for the contemporary notion of "thing" which grounds human affairs on this earth as synecdoche, represents and calls forward the ancient image of the bounded place in the Icelandic history, the Thing. In Peircean semiotics Thing-ness is that sign function which mediates between image and code, between Icon and Symbol. Peirce implicitly draws upon the rich heritage of the Thing in Common Law and thus understands, interpretively, that the Thing, evolved from the judgment place of the sagas, is represented by the sign function of Indexicality. The Index, in this semiotic schema, characterizes opposition, interaction, experience.

Third, for me, in a very special way, Pencak's study of the Icelandic sagas, from the perspective of a semiotician and historian, recollects a time long passed in my own development when I had been a writer of poems, plays, and fiction and had written a novel that took place in Iceland. I had never visited Iceland until the 1993 International Congress for the Philosophy of Law and Social Philosophy in Reykjavik, but had taken my material on Things from *National Geographic* and elsewhere. That novel had been centered on "survival," on conflicts of survival, and thus on conflicts of legal and legitimate codes. The 1993 visit to Iceland, profoundly enhanced by Pencak's study here, gave me a rare opportunity to recall some of the old things of myself, to see them and to know the role they had played in this the person I have come to be.

This triad of pleasures in Pencak's Icelandic text is good to share, as I share, also, a few ideas on the work in itself:

Pencak argues — indeed, his overarching thesis is — that the Icelandic sagas provide us with the Icelandic *thing* as a pluralistic, even anarchistic, self-shaping means of settling disputes in lawful fashion. This means then fell apart "when aristocratic factions began to corrupt them" (p. 2).

Pencak shows that the sagas were quasi-historical representations of Icelandic law and justice; they interpretively signified the historical development of a people. The actual referent of the historical narrative of the sagas is disclosed by means of two predominant yet distinct modes of literary "distortion." One such mode is condensation, such that the sagas are, on one level, "tales which compress the history of the Icelandic republic into a shorter span." The other mode, Pencak points out, is a counterpart; it constitutes a continuum theme of struggle. On the one hand, feuds are resolved by having recourse to customary law and to the collective will of the people, and thus result in a kind of "felt justice." But on the other hand, and more increasingly, authority outside the society is called upon to serve as arbiter of justice; thus the sagas come to cross their own boundaries, as it were, as the quest for justice becomes a *trek* or pilgrimage. Pencak says, Iceland's "submission to an overseas church and state as a means of ending its tragic feuds" coincides with the transition from ancient to a new kind of law (p. 4).

Interpretation of the sagas, as Pencak notes, fits excellently with some approaches of legal semiotics; for example, the leading metaphors of the sagas, such as "the battlefield," become in turn "Immediate Interpretant Signs" (in Peircean sense) that lead to, and become the possibility for emergent symbolic judgments (p. 4).

Further, unlike traditional approaches to explaining law as a command (a deontic structure) imposed on a jural society from without, Pencak observes that a legal semiotics would interpret Icelandic law, as signified by the sagas in part, as an exchange and a confrontational process of question and answer (p. 5).

This is only one of several ways that Pencak offers as examples of how the sagas disclose not only ways of seeing the law, but also of "things" of law as representations of conditions of human social life.

It is Pencak's achievement to recover the living ideas that are contextually framed within the sagas; this achievement is analogous with the discovery of a kind of "deep structure" still resident in our languages, our speech, and our gestures. Peirce writes of these isomorphs, and explicitly discusses the "thing" in connection with prescinding an object of inquiry from its usual context, its ground, in order to free it from connotations, from vestigial meaning (Peirce, Ms. 105, Harvard Lectures VIII). Again, Representations stand for Things, that is, for judgments of an existential (opposed to hypothetical) kind (1865, above, reprinted in WoP I: pp. 256-257; 274-275).

Nearly twenty years have passed since I first introduced Legal Semiotics with my *Inlaws/Outlaws* (1977), where I called attention to the evolution of the Icelandic Thing into Anglo-Commonlaw, such that the "thing" becomes a legal frame or "play space" in which to stage enactments of disputes (Kevelson 1977: 4-5).

Many studies of English Commonlaw speak of its Icelandic legacies (see the classic Gunmere, 1930: 192, 332). Gunmere especially notes the equal role of women in Icelandic law, which diminishes as the power for self-determination shifts from internal authority to external authority. Pencak suggests that Icelandic legal stability and self-governing power declined in direct proportion to the decline of women's equality as the feudal subordination of women, along with the rest of feudalism's hierarchical structure, became adapted by the Icelandic peoples (p. 2).

Pencak's "voice-over" in this remarkable study of the Icelandic sagas shows these tales as ways of understanding the many dimensions of their world: "they probed their subject from several perspectives, painted a canvas as complicated and vast as the reality they described" (p. 128).

This, too, can be said of Bill Pencak's own special way of viewing: of giving us full this panoramic chiaroscuro in high relief.

Roberta Kevelson
Distinguished Professor of Philosophy
Director, Center in Semiotic Research
August 1994

REFERENCES

Gunmere, F.B., 1930, *Founders of England*, New York: G.E. Stechart & Co.

Kevelson, R., 1977, *Inlaws/Outlaws: A Semiotics of Systemic Interaction*, Bloomington and Lisse: R.C.L.S.S. with Peter de Ridder Press.

Peirce, Charles Sanders, Microfilm Edition, Ms. 105, reprinted in *Writings of Charles S. Peirce*, I, eds. M. Fisch *et al.*, Bloomington: Indiana University Press.

AUTHOR'S PREFACE

During the two millennia which separate the tragedies of Aeschylus, Sophocles, and Euripides from those of Shakespeare stands only one comparable body of literature: the great Icelandic sagas of the thirteenth century. If ever evidence is needed to show that societies which foster personal freedom also produce the finest works of the human mind, medieval Iceland may proudly raise its head alongside classical Greece and Renaissance England. It is no wonder that the respective populations of all three societies have celebrated these epic masterpieces as the essence of their civilizations. Here are no anonymous masses reduced to spectators and supporters of kings, nobles, and prophets, as found in most Roman, Biblical, and medieval writings, heroes too superhuman or demoniacal to be believable, too one-dimensional to resonate with real life. The incidents of the sagas, the great scholar W. P. Ker has written, "are not such wonders as to be outside the bounds of common experience." Ker notes that "the sagas differ from all other 'heroic' literatures in the larger proportion that they give to the meanness of reality."[1] In the sagas, as in the Greek and Renaissance English plays, the mighty are humanized. Oedipus and Phaedra, Hamlet and Othello, the Greek chorus and Shakespeare's common folk have come to symbolize fundamental struggles in the human psyche and socio-political world. So too, were they better known, would Njal and Gunnar, Egil and Snorri, Grettir and Gudrun.

Like the Greek and Shakespearean tragedies, the Icelandic sagas are not history, which professional historians delude themselves is the effort to describe the past accurately, but the more realistic attempt to meditate on the significance of the past for the present. This is what historians in fact do, although usually in spite of themselves. Prepared for audiences of Icelanders in the thirteenth century as their republic was collapsing after four hundred years, the sagas are not only great stories, but invitations to critical reflection on the fate of a unique republic. At issue are conflicting visions of law, justice, social order, and individuality.

My short essays on sagas which have been the focus of entire books by no means exhaust their subjects. I gratefully acknowledge the work of W. P. Ker, Theodore Andersson, Carol Clover, Jesse Byock, Hermann Pálsson, Paul Edwards, Magnus Magnusson, Lars Lönnroth, Einar Sveinsson, Richard F. Allen, and Paul Schach for providing me with the introduction to Icelandic history and literature I needed to undertake my work. The work of William Ian Miller on Icelandic law has been especially illuminating, although he is more interested in using the sagas to understand what Icelandic law was really like, while I am more concerned with using what we know about Icelandic history to understand the timeless legal and ethical issues which the sagas raise and which endow them with greatness.[2]

I am not a reader of Icelandic: the translations I arrived at were based on comparing various English versions of the sagas. Scholars well-versed in the extensive Icelandic and Germanic literature on the sagas may object that I am poaching on their territory. My defense is that if the sagas are to reach a large audience and their stature as great literature be made more widely known, they need to be read much as Plato, the *Bible*, or Don Quixote are by philosophers and literary critics to reveal insights into the common adventure of humanity.

I owe the genesis of this book to two remarkable friends — Roberta Kevelson and Robert Ginsberg, my colleagues in the Philosophy Department at Penn State. Professor Kevelson invited me to present a paper on legal semiotics at the 1993 conference of the International Association for Philosophy of Law and Social Philosophy. Since the meeting was held in Reykjavik, Iceland, I thought it would be appropriate to apply semiotic insights to the great body of Icelandic literature which deals so richly with legal and ethical questions. Unfortunately, I was unable to attend the conference, but once I began thinking about the sagas, I could not stop writing. They have attracted me as no other writings since I discovered the Greek classics in college a quarter-century ago. If this book has a subtext it is to convey the intellectual as well as aesthetic excitement of a body of literature second-to-none, to those who have not yet read it. Hence, when Robert Ginsberg suggested I contribute a volume to the Value Inquiry Book Series, which he edits for Rodopi, I did not have to search for a topic.

I thank Cindy Palecek and her staff at "A Perfect Secretary," Reading, Pennsylvania, for preparing a most attractive book. Gary Gallagher, Chair of the History Department at the Pennsylvania State University arranged for me to spend the spring semester of 1993 at University Park which enabled me to write the book. His friendship and encouragement of my work have been very important to me. The Commonwealth Educational System research office and Ogontz Campus, respectively headed by Jack Royer and Leonard Mustazza, supported the publication of this book both financially and spiritually, as they have done with much of my work. My great thanks to these wonderful people.

Aside from the encouragement of Professors Kevelson and Ginsberg, the members of the Penn State Round Table for Law and Semiotics, especially my good friends Virginia Black, Manfred Pieck, and the late Gordon Whitney, have been the kindest and most incisive of critics. Two Icelandic scholars, Mikail Karlsson of the University of Iceland and Nancy Brown of my own university, persuaded me to make key improvements in the text, which they were kind enough to read in its entirety. Professor S. Leonard Rubinstein of Penn State made several astute comments when he interviewed me concerning this book for the Comparative Literature Department's ''Odyssey Through Literature'' radio show for WPSX, State College. Jeff Polizzotto, who would make a wonderful Icelandic hero himself, provided a good deal of the moral support I needed to finish this book. Patrick J. Stevens, curator of the Fiske Collection of Icelandic Materials at Cornell University provided friendly and invaluable assistance in selecting the illustrations, all of which appear courtesy of the Rare Books and Manuscripts Division of the Kroch Library at Cornell. My parents, Charles and Harriett Pencak, have been a never-failing source of whatever financial help I have needed to do my work. Their love for an eccentric scholar has also been boundless. The dedication is for them, too.

Glenside, Pennsylvania

Chapter One

INTRODUCTION: THE HISTORICAL AND PHILOSOPHICAL CONTEXT

Medieval Iceland is perhaps the closest approximation of an anarchist or libertarian republic that the world is likely to see. Founded in the years between 870 and 930, when its Althing and legal system were established, Iceland was settled by people unwilling to submit to a more coercive and, as the sagas describe it, tyrannical Norwegian monarchy. They divided the new land into four quarters, each of which had three local "Things" or courts as well as its Quarter Court. (A fifth appeals court was added later to break deadlocks). The Althing, a combination supreme court and legislative body, met for two weeks each year in the middle of the summer. Every "thing man" in the land, some 4,500 in all by 1100, could attend the Althing and serve as a judge in a legal case. Iceland had no ruler and only one paid official, the Law-Speaker, whose task it was to recite the law over a three-year period and, with the advice of recognized experts, inform people what the law was in hard cases.[1]

The law and the Things bound Iceland together. Religion did not. Pagan temples, and, after Iceland adopted Christianity in 1000, churches were owned by local notables: only in the period of the republic's decline, beginning in the late twelfth century, did the Roman Catholic hierarchy acquire wealth and power. Iceland also had no army or navy, as no one threatened its independence. Although the sagas tell us fish and timber were plentiful during the republic's early years, the land was quickly settled and resources soon became scarce. Most of Iceland is composed of glaciers or volcanic rock unfit for settlement: the soil could not support much agriculture, and people lived chiefly on meat, fish, and dairy products. The first settlers soon depleted Iceland's supply of usable timber, and most houses were built of turf. Wealthy people traveled to Norway to obtain timber for dwellings and churches.

At its peak, medieval Iceland had between 50,000 and 100,000 inhabitants. There were no towns or even villages. The population was divided into households headed by free farmers, or bonders, which included servants, slaves, foster-kin, and various relatives. Extended kinship ties were also important: there were numerous blood brothers and foster children. Each farmer attached himself to a chief, whose responsible behavior was ensured by the fact that his men could simply leave and join another of the fifty or so chieftains in the country. In practice, however, which chief a man joined depended on the power structure of a region: men swore allegiance to a chief who would take their part in disputes over land, fish, inheritance, animals, etc. In return, they would accompany him to the local Things and Althing and support his cases.

Women enjoyed a much higher status than usual in the early republic. They could inherit property, divorce husbands at will — the reverse was also true — and head households. Men exercised women's legal rights by proxy, but the sagas reveal women to be influential community leaders for both good and ill. Carol Clover has explained women's exalted position in Iceland as arising from its status as a typical frontier community, where men far outnumbered women, thus conferring high status on the few desirable, wealthy women available for marriage. Female infanticide also reduced their numbers. Jenny Jochens has disputed Clover's findings, arguing that in the *Sturlunga Saga* dealing with Icelandic life in the twelfth and thirteenth centuries women are not consulted on their marriage partners, divorcing their husbands, or deciding political matters. Yet Clover argues convincingly that the sagas must have some basis in Icelandic social reality — such a unique literature could not have come out of nothing. Furthermore, Jochens's examples are from later times, when Iceland was becoming more aristocratic and unstable, and when women, too, were being reduced in status to the more general level of feudal Europe.[2]

Besides honoring women to a remarkable degree, Iceland had many types of law and justice. A disgruntled citizen could attack his opponent and kill him, satisfying the deceased's kin with either monetary or in-kind compensation (animals, spun cloth). If the relatives were not satisfied, they could attack and kill him in turn. But either party also had the option of taking a case to court or submitting it informally to respected arbiters. Courts could outlaw troublemakers for three years (usually) or life (in exceptional cases) or award compensation to the party perceived to be injured. Through most of Iceland's history Thing justice dispensed by the courts worked reasonably well, only falling apart when aristocratic factions began to corrupt them. Through the presence of large numbers of armed followers, the chiefs turned the courts into battlegrounds as the republic approached its end.

Most Icelandic quarrels were over scarce resources: wood, beached whales, fish, grazing rights, and animals. More infrequently, inheritances and sheer arrogance would cause people to argue, although these two factors figure prominently in the great family sagas. The central issues of these sagas are: can the legal system represented by the courts do justice, and can it keep the peace and preserve the Icelandic republic? These goals were not always compatible, as Grettir's unjust outlawry graphically shows. Iceland and its sagas depict a nation of free men, abetted by formidable women, testing conflicting legal codes — vengeance vs. compromise, pagan vs. Christian, formal vs. informal, monarchical (Norwegian) vs. republican (Icelandic). The sagas I discuss in this book reveal the types of people who emerged in the republic — an impulsive hero, a cautious sage, an unjustly persecuted outlaw, some powerful women, a poet, a politically astute manipulator, merchants in conflict with chiefs — and show their development as the sagas compress the founding, maturing, weakening, and dissolution of Iceland's autonomous institutions into single lifetimes.

Although ostensibly set in the tenth century and dealing with the period of Iceland's founding, the sagas I treat here build freely on historical facts to consider the problem of why the republic fell apart in the thirteenth century.[3] Njal, for instance, was an obscure farmer rather than the greatest law advocate in Icelandic history. The author of his saga used the horrible means of his death to illustrate the destruction of the legal system whose spirit Njal represents, and its deterioration into martial combat, which only occurred long after the historical Njal's death.

Theodore Andersson has elucidated a basic structure for all the sagas I discuss, as well as many others; an *introduction* provides the background and presents the characters and issues, usually going back at least a generation, which propel the saga's action; *conflict* arises, which builds to a destructive *climax*; *revenge* is taken for the death of the saga's hero, and a *reconciliation* is arranged.[4] I would expand Andersson's typology in two ways. First, if we regard the sagas as tales which compress the history of the Icelandic republic into a shorter span, the introduction usually sets forth the way republican justice, properly functioning during the years of Iceland's founding, could successfully solve problems that prove intractable and disastrous in the main body of the saga. (The exception is *Egil's Saga*, which does the reverse: it shows how the Norwegian monarchy cannot do justice or achieve peace, whereas the Icelandic republic, symbolized by the transformation of the fierce viking

Egil into a poet and patriarch, can do both). Second, many of the sagas end with pilgrimages to Rome and voyages to Norway, symbolizing the republic's submission to an overseas church and state as the means of ending its tragic feuds.

The greatness of the sagas lies in the fact that their authors do not present oversimplified cases either for the glory of republican Iceland or the inadequacies of monarchy. Through the "signs" of characters and events which develop complexly as the republic evolves, pros and cons of different types of behavior and different theories of law and justice are presented with great subtlety. This leaves it to the readers to recapitulate the sagas' own intellectual task and judge the worth of the republic and its competitors for themselves. Alternative interpretations of the merits of clerical and monarchical authority, of the efficacy of Thing justice, of the ability of the Icelandic republic to act morally while keeping the peace, of the validity of stepping outside the law to do real justice when legal technicalities stand in the way are constantly arising. For example, was Iceland's submission to Norway in 1262 a satisfactory conclusion to anarchy and civil war, a bad solution but the best one available, a judgment on the inability of the republic to preserve order, or the sad end of a great experiment in self-government? Were Iceland's great women its glory, or a curse which egged on the feuds that precipitated the republic's demise? Under what conditions can exceptional people put their talents to use for the common good, and under what circumstances will they be tragically destroyed by their own excellence? The sagas are constantly probing such questions.

I have selected these "family" sagas out of the many tales produced by Icelanders in the days of their republic's decline and after its destruction because they deal with universal legal and moral issues in the most detailed, sophisticated, and interesting manner. If this book has scholarly value, it is because I am applying the methodology of legal semiotics to a body of literature that cries out for such an approach. Legal semiotics looks at law not as authoritative, or as a set of texts with definitive status, but rather as an amorphous field — we might use the metaphor of battlefield — where different communities of interpreters — judges, lawyers, scholars, legislators, interested citizens — interact to create "the law" in accordance with their needs and expertise. Given this approach, statutes, judicial decisions, legal language, and the interpreters themselves emerge as "signs" of legal and ethical codes which are always changing through their mutual interaction. Once we realize that law, like history or life itself, cannot be frozen, then people take on the freedom of active participants in the adventure of shaping the moral and judicial norms which will in turn symbolize their behavior.[5]

Any legal system can be profitably studied semiotically, for even "totalitarian" societies have loopholes and generate their own subversion, but in medieval Iceland the evolution of a republic of free people, creating law from a welter of possibilities, makes such an approach exceptionally fruitful. A semiotic perspective can solve some problems of interpreting the sagas. For instance, "was Njal a good man" is no longer answered with "yes" or "no," but by a spectrum of possibilities. Semiotics allows use of the sagas as evidence to evaluate the philosophies of law articulated by legal theorists.

Medieval Iceland was that rare nation relatively isolated from the rest of the world (except when its people went raiding or travelling) and therefore free to create whatever legal institutions it chose. (The Founding Fathers of the United States enjoyed a similar prospect in 1787.) In the course of four centuries after 870 A.D., the Icelanders tried nearly every form of law discussed by Western civilization since ancient times. This bleak, remote North Atlantic island of under 100,000 souls presents us with a laboratory for experiments in legal philosophy, a microcosm of the world through which we may study the possibilities and limitations of types of law which have surfaced throughout history.

Legal philosophy can take at least five directions.[6] It may look at what *principles* validate law and compel obedience; it may examine what *procedures* best do justice; or it may inquire into what should be the *purposes* of law. The two other directions — establishing the best form of government and determining the conditions under which republics can survive — I will arbitrarily assign to "political" rather than "legal" philosophy so my book may have a conclusion.

Natural law, positive law, traditional or customary law, and pragmatic jurisprudence (sometimes known as "legal realism") are the four basic philosophies which have been offered as to why people should obey the law. (A semiotic approach, on the other hand, does not stipulate whether people should obey the law or not; it examines different interpretations of the laws and reasons for adhering to them or disobeying them).

Natural law insists that law conform to universal principles of morality or justice, fixed by God, human nature, or the constitution of the universe. An unjust law is no law, St. Thomas Aquinas approvingly cited

St. Augustine. In recent times C. S. Lewis has shown that all the world's higher religions and civilizations have similar underlying laws, such as those preserving families (however different their structures), prohibiting theft and murder within society, and requiring obedience to properly constituted authority.[7] On the other hand, advocates of positive law, following John Austin and H. L. A. Hart, only admit to *coincidences* between moral injunctions and legal rules. They insist that what makes "law" is not its agreement with universal moral principles but the command of a sovereign recognized as authoritative within a given society.[8] Ronald Dworkin has to some extent synthesized natural and positive law by showing moral arguments are specified or implied in many, if not all, laws. Judges are required, in positive law, to exercise moral judgment in reaching decisions, as in determining appropriate sentences for criminals.[9] Sovereignty, too, is problematic, as it always claims moral as well as legal foundations. And it is not absolutely authoritative. All states have formal chains of command, informal mechanisms of control, and enforcement agencies which may work at cross purposes.

"Rights," Edmund Burke noted, "are in a sort of middle [we might even say muddle], incapable of being defined, but not impossible to be discerned."[10] Between a natural law requiring positive law for enforcement and a positive law requiring overlap with natural law for popular legitimacy lie three mediating alternatives: utility, custom, and pragmatic change. Utility, defined by John Stuart Mill as "the greatest good of the greatest number," is one yardstick.[11] But who is numbered and what is good? Material happiness (how much?) or a virtuous community of saints and scholars? Should everyone have a basic modicum of happiness, or should the well-being of those presumed more capable of doing good to others receive preference? Mill himself was well aware that utility, like natural law, was an overarching principle which did not dictate its own enforcement in specific instances.

Traditional law may be defined as the informal bundle of laws and legitimate, though not legally codified, customs which explain the real behavior of a society. It stresses maintenance of order and preservation of institutions as a primary goal, arguing that attempts to reorganize a state according to abstract principles usually leads to disaster.[12] But except in the most homogeneous societies, traditions conflict and are subject to interpretation. In eighteenth century Europe, church, nobility, monarchy, and the bourgeoisie all claimed traditional sanction for their privileges: the conflicts among them opened the door to the French Revolution. In the United States today, nearly all judges claim to revere "the Constitution" while disagreeing over what statutes and modes of interpretation are legitimate. Traditions are not so much inherited as constantly recreated to accord with perceived, present needs.

Hence we arrive at pragmatic jurisprudence, or legal realism, which has the opposite problem as traditional law. It states that law should be and is adapted to changing social circumstances.[13] But at the same time, except in extreme revolutionary situations, and perhaps not even there, reinterpretation occurs within traditional limits and on grounds of precedent. There is always the question of whose needs should be given priority in a changing society, and what are the best legal devices for ensuring this is done. *Brown vs. Board of Education* tells us to integrate public schools "with all deliberate speed," but it does not provide a blueprint or timetable for every school district in the United States.

The Icelandic sagas demonstrate that their authors were pondering the advantages and disadvantages of these four philosophies of law from a semiotic perspective. Of course, they did not use the technical jargon of twentieth-century philosophy, which is why they will remain fresh and profound long after our legal theorists have changed their terminology. But no other nation, to my knowledge, has given the problem of legal institutions so central a place in its literature, or examined them from so many points of view with all the advantages and drawbacks of each presented so thoroughly or poignantly. Iceland's writers, much like the founders of the American nation, were acutely aware of the uniqueness of their republican experiment. Like critics of American institutions from Herman Melville to Herbert Marcuse, they agonized deeply over the fate of a republic which they believed had deserted its principles and lost its freedom.

At first glance, the sagas seem to state that a corrupted Iceland's positive law has repudiated morality or natural law. For instance, *Njal's Saga* opens with a case where a man learned in the law corrupts justice to win his daughter an inheritance against common sense fairness. The ruling offends the community, so the Althing permits a challenge of combat to our "shyster lawyer," who loses the money if not the case. This episode is a prelude to the saga's main action — Njal, Iceland's most respected legal sage, is burned to death in his house with his family after he has made a last-ditch effort to save the legal system. When the killers are acquitted on a trivial technical point, law collapses as the Althing becomes a battleground.

Grettir's Saga poses a similar dilemma. Grettir is an unpleasant bully, but ironically he is outlawed for the unfortunate consequences of a good deed. He appears at a house during a storm seeking aid for his shipwrecked companions, but is attacked by those within — whom he kills — because he looks like a troll. Much of the saga deals with Grettir's unjust sufferings and the havoc he must wreak on the community in order to survive during his undeserved outlawry. The situation is even more outrageous because the outlawry itself is illegal — Grettir killed the people in Norway — and only occurs when a powerful man corrupts the Althing.

Bandamanna Saga and the story of "Ale-Hood" also have us rooting for underdogs representing natural law. Ordinary Icelanders take advantage of divisions among the island's great chiefs who are manipulating the Althing to deprive them unjustly of their property. The commoners must use knavery to combat knavery, but do so in the name of justice. *Eyrbyggja Saga* presents the same problem on a more deadly level. Unable to settle disputes at the Althing, the chiefs fight it out and need to be saved by the intervention of the community at large.

The sagas thus make a strong case for natural law as the necessary bulwark of positive law in order for the latter to be enforced in Iceland's free society. But the sagas also show that in many instances it is impossible to discover where justice resides. For instance, Njal's otherwise laudable effort to save a legal system that has deadlocked through repeated manipulations of jurors is flawed. He has set up the Fifth Court of Appeals with the ulterior motive of securing a chieftainship for his foster-son Hoskuld so the man may marry a prominent woman who will not settle for less than a chief. Njal's favoritism spurs his natural sons to kill Hoskuld, which in turn provokes Hoskuld's kin to burn Njal's family. The protracted vendetta only comes to an end when Flosi, the leader of Njal's enemies, decides to submit to the vengeance of Kari, the surviving head of Njal's clan, in a spirit of Christian forgiveness.

Yet the saga does not tell us "Christianity is the answer" either, for Christian behavior is no less ambiguous than law or justice. The Valkyries reappear at the end of *Njal's Saga* and blood flows on an Icelandic priest celebrating Easter Mass. Earlier in the saga, Amundi the Blind had prayed to the Christian God, immediately after Iceland embraced the new faith, to open his eyes for an instant that he may slay his father's murderer, even though compensation has been paid and the case settled at the Althing. God obliges. Flosi and his accomplices went to mass just before incinerating Njal and his family. Christianity embraces extreme forms of revenge and forgiveness that were both rejected by an Icelandic legal system which emphasized the compromise settling of disputes through paying compensation or outlawing unruly characters who threatened the peace.

Sometimes the sagas appear clear as to where true justice lies. When Grettir pleads for a trial in Norway, even the king, St. Olaf, refuses and banishes him from the kingdom. Egil, too, is about to receive a trial in Norway to determine if he killed in self-defense, when Queen Gunnhild orders her henchmen to cut the ropes defining the court's boundaries into which weapons may not be brought. Egil escapes his pursuers. But even here the cases are complicated: Grettir had impetuously slain a lad who advised the king not to try him, and a friend of Egil had fixed the Norwegian jury to ensure his innocence. The sagas may be suggesting that even the arbitrary judgment of Norwegian monarchs was preferable to Icelanders who have a fine legal system but did not abide by it. Or the contrary may be true — the abortive trials of Grettir and Egil may imply that monarchs rarely do justice, thereby vindicating Iceland's existence as a republic comprised of those who fled Norwegian tyranny. Or the trials may point to the need for Norway to reassert its authority to end Iceland's internal anarchy. All the major sagas present us with complicated chains of vengeance-seeking which become so tangled that it is impossible to decide where true justice may be found.

Utility, custom, and legal realism are also tested in the sagas. The outlawry of Gunnar in *Njal's Saga* is a question of pure utility: Gunnar has repeatedly been declared innocent of murder by reason of self-defense at the Althing. But his boastfulness is constantly stirring up fights, so he is outlawed for three years. Gunnar may be interpreted as either an intrepid champion of justice and honor, or an arrogant troublemaker unconcerned with the general welfare. In the *Laxdaela Saga*, the Althing makes a belated appearance near the end to wind up a quarrel when Gudrun finally thinks she has taken adequate blood-vengeance for her husband's murder. Egil secures at the Althing the banishment of a man who is tormenting his son on the grounds his exile is useful for peace in the region. The sad tale of *Gunnlaug Worm-Tongue*, a sequel of sorts to *Egil's Saga,* demonstrates the consequences when arch-rivals Gunnlaug and Hrafn insist on fighting to the death. They follow each other all over Iceland and Scandinavia until they finally duel over the woman they both love; the result is a horrible struggle in which they hack each other to pieces.

Customary law is most effective in the early chapters of the sagas. In most cases these passages discuss the establishment of Iceland. Before the Althing was created — and material resources were plentiful, the texts emphasize repeatedly — great chiefs reached informal agreements to divide land, share food, and settle disputes equitably. The sagas look back wistfully to this era. Residues of the founding age appear when chiefs stop feuds: Kari and Flosi reconcile their differences, and the two sides in the climactic battle of *Eyrbyggja Saga* cease fighting when one chief realizes his grandson is in the opposing camp. Egil the warrior-poet in Norway becomes the patriarch and bard of friendship and affection in Iceland. Yet in most cases, only terrible events like the burning of Njal, Grettir's outlawry, Gudrun's protracted vengeance, and the death of Snorri's opponents in *Eyrbyggja Saga* compel the latter-day chiefs to open their eyes and seek peace.

Formal law also changes in Iceland in accord with pragmatic jurisprudence. Njal is at times a legal realist, persuading the Althing to create a new court of appeals when the system is breaking down. Gunnlaug's and Hrafn's rivalry leads to the outlawing of personal duels to settle disputes in both Iceland and Norway. Grettir's death causes the old pagan religion, which the Christian majority had previously tolerated, to be banned because a curse caused his demise. At the beginning of *Eyrbyggja Saga*, a pagan temple is transformed into a law court when two powerful chiefs dispute access to the place, symbolizing how Iceland made law, rather than religion, the basis of its civilization.

Like Christianity, the old pagan religion of Odin and Thor gets mixed reviews in the sagas. If Christianity generates the curse which destroys Grettir, Egil is the pagan champion of justice against a Christian tyrant. Neither Christianity nor the old Norse gods, like the law itself, stands unambiguously for justice or injustice.

The Icelandic sagas, then, do not dictate which code of law we should obey or why we should obey it. Like contemporary semiotics, they present a conflict among legal practices and principles, uneasily coexisting or in outright opposition, which command greater or lesser respect depending on context and circumstance.

The sagas are equally enigmatic in evaluating the procedures available for doing justice. All have their strengths and weaknesses. The most satisfactory solution, where great men informally work out agreements so there is no need for either court disputes or pitched battles, is also the most ephemeral. It only works during the brief period of Iceland's settlement when resources are plentiful. It becomes the worst solution later, for the chiefs corrupt the Althing and ignore its rulings, preferring to fight it out, in the main events of the sagas. When they finally reconcile, either the community has compelled them or they are exhausted after long chains of vendettas.

Blood revenge, either a challenge to single combat or undertaken by a band of men, was also legal in Iceland, provided the victim's family was satisfactorily compensated. However, as *Njal's Saga* graphically illustrates, such feuds escalate and eventually finish up at the Althing, which has a harder time settling them the more bloody they become. The Althing works sometimes in the sagas to stop violence through negotiation, mandated monetary compensation, or outlawry. But the sagas note the legislature's inability to keep the peace once social strife among the great chiefs has corrupted its procedures: verdicts are either won on technicalities or are simply ignored.

The sagas leave the possibility of Christian forgiveness and monarchical justice open as solutions for Iceland's internal quarrels. Christianity is identified with the foreign Norwegian king who is usually portrayed as a tyrant. Neither the Christian church nor the king brings true justice to Iceland: they require both individuals and the entire republic to sacrifice their rights. Yet whether church and crown are harmful alien impositions or the best solutions available to a nation torn by strife is an unanswerable question the sagas pose for us through the people who support and resist their innovations.

The true purpose of law is another puzzle the sagas let us solve for ourselves. Should law exact strict personal justice — an eye for an eye — or should justice be tempered in the interest of keeping the peace and thus improving the conditions under which everyone must live? Republican Iceland offered the alternatives of monetary compensation for deaths and injuries, outlawing of troublesome individuals regardless of who was strictly accountable for violence, and Christian mercy. But while the community strove mightily to control quarrelsome people and stop feuds through these means, all had their drawbacks. Compensation failed to satisfy victims' kin, outlaws such as Gunnar and Grettir refused to leave the country, and mercy sometimes went unappreciated: forgiveness usually occurred after terrifying battles and vendettas which dragged on for years. Like toleration in modern Europe, which gained adherents after the bloody sixteenth and seventeenth century wars of religion, Icelanders forgave each other as an alternative to mutual suicide.

Despite the outlet which many individuals took, of travelling to Norway or elsewhere to let off steam and fight like the vikings of old, Icelanders lacked a common external enemy against whom they could unite in a heroic struggle. On the European continent, Scandinavians of a similar temperament invaded France, England, Sicily, Russia, and served as the Byzantine Emperor's Varangian Guard.

But Iceland could only turn inward. As the republic destroyed itself, it began to think about its astonishing history — how free men had tried to rule themselves without coercive authority, only to descend into aristocratic feuding and finally submit to an absolute foreign monarch supported by a state church. Like Thucydides bewailing the destruction of Periclean Athenian democracy or Tacitus mourning the decline of the Roman republic, the sagas' authors looked unblinkingly at both the faults and virtues of the country they loved. In so doing, they assured medieval Iceland of immortality, and left citizens of future republics the opportunity to think deeply about whether law — and what sort of law — can coincide with justice.

Chapter Two

THE HERO AND THE SAGE: *NJAL'S SAGA*

Synopsis: The households of Njal and Gunnar, respectively the wisest and most valiant man in Iceland, feud despite their personal friendship and efforts to keep peace. Their wives Bergthora and Hallgerd spur on the feud, which ends in the deaths of Gunnar and Njal. The collapse of Iceland's legal system follows, as Njal's murderers escape on a technicality and the Althing degenerates into a battleground. Flosi, who led the burners of Njal's house, and Kari, Njal's avenger, are ultimately reconciled.

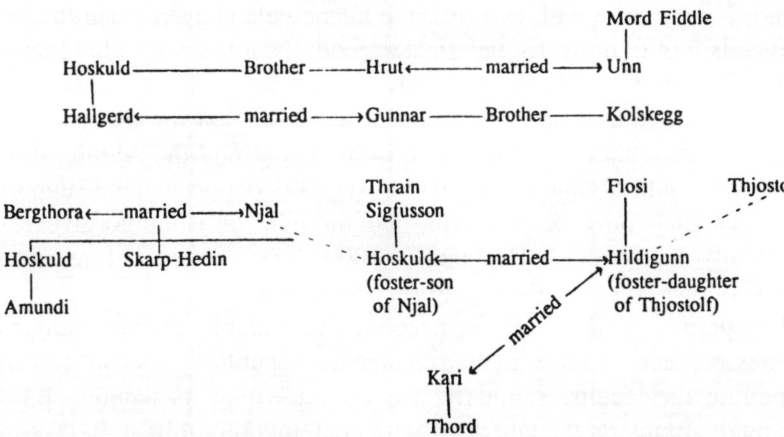

Njal's Saga invites comparison with Thucydides' *The Peloponnesian War* as the tragedy of a great republic destroying itself. Not content with laurels won defeating the Persians and establishing a wealthy city and unprecedented culture, Athens came to grief when it sought to enhance its reputation by conquering other states. Unwilling to compromise their honor, temper, and sense of justice through the fragile legal institutions they erected to preserve order, Icelanders literally turned their courts into battlegrounds rather than surrender their principles or injure their pride. The saga writers and Greek sages both knew, hubris was the downfall of societies and individuals. If we see the tragedy of Athens writ microcosmically in the lives of Pericles, Alcibiades, and Nicias, the fates of Njal, Gunnar, Kari, and Flosi humanize and stand for the demise of one of those rare pre-modern republics which heroically attempted to balance might and right.

Njal's Saga is the tragedy of Gunnar, the bravest and noblest man in Iceland, and his best friend Njal, the wisest and most learned in the law. Between them they represent the best of the recently demolished republic, for the saga was probably written within a decade of the Althing's abolition in 1271.[1] Their embodiment as the essence of republican Iceland is reinforced by the fact that Njal was born in 930, the date the Althing was founded, and was murdered when his efforts to keep peace through that body ceased to work. Similarly, Gunnar offers the only paean to the natural beauty of Iceland in any of the major sagas, thereby uniquely identifying himself with the country.

Both Njal and Gunnar are destroyed by their greatest virtue. Gunnar will not compromise with evil or leave his homeland even when the law commands him to do so for the greater good. Njal is loyal to his friends and family even when they act unjustly, and continues his efforts to make peace through the legal system even when he knows the cause is hopeless. After Njal is burned alive in his house and the Althing itself breaks down into a violent struggle between his opponents and supporters, peace may only be re-established through Christian forgiveness. Christianity had come to Iceland in 1000 A.D. — just before doom descends upon Njal and the legal order he represents.

Interpreting *Njal's Saga* as a condensed parable of the strengths, weaknesses, and demise of the Icelandic republic goes far toward reconciling the leading scholarly debate concerning its nature. Bardi Gudmundsson insists the tale deals with contemporary thirteenth-century events — while only incidentally borrowing tenth-century materials — whereas Einar Sveinsson regards it as based primarily on authentic incidents handed down by oral tradition.[2] If Njal and his role as a signifier of the land and its law are understood, it can be shown that the saga's author poured several centuries of the feuds, reconciliations, and legal history of Iceland into one man's life and experiences. He did so to test the hypothesis whether law can govern the passions and do justice in a free, consensual society.

But there are no definitive answers, either for Njal's republic or for any other. The saga may be interpreted in at least two ways. One, Njal

Gunnar, the Althing, and the other characters may symbolize an Icelandic legal system that was good and functional — it endured for 340 years — only to be destroyed by the ungovernable tempers and eventual corruption of the volatile population. It yielded to two alternative, unsatisfactory resolutions, first, total anarchy, then subservience to foreign political and clerical domination from Norway and Rome, respectively. On the other hand, given the feuds and murders present from Iceland's founding which the Althing was always hard pressed to handle, the saga may be pointing out the inherent instability and inadequacy of the old republic, thereby implicitly arguing for the superiority of the Christian monarchy imported recently from Norway to end the turmoil. At least some credence is owed this interpretation, for *Njal's Saga* originated in the Svinafell region in southern Iceland where descendants of Flosi, who had led the burners of Njal's house, were the leading family. In the saga, the hitherto reviled man is rehabilitated as a noble soul who only reluctantly leads the attack after considerable provocation, and then achieves through personal forbearance the peace Njal could not arrange through the law.[3]

Undoubtedly Icelanders argued passionately for both interpretations around their firesides on those long winter nights when the saga was declaimed. We may still do so today, for the characters, situations, and institutions it portrays embody the great ethical questions which perpetually vex humankind. Is freedom compatible with social stability? Can people govern themselves consensually? Is law compatible with justice, or should it be more concerned with compromise for the sake of peacekeeping? There are no easy answers to these questions in *Njal's Saga*: there could not be or the dilemmas and tragedies of its characters would not ring so true after seven centuries. Instead, we are provided the opportunity to share their quest for an ethical political order. To borrow Einar Sveinsson's eloquent words:

> My attempt to investigate the genesis of a work like *Njal's Saga*, where so much is and will always remain obscure, is not unlike trying to explore the vastness of space with a flashlight on a dark and cloudy autumn night. Such attempts can be intriguing and exciting, but because of the inescapable uncertainty of the results they can never be intellectually satisfying. One "perhaps" is piled upon another, and even the most ingeniously contrived hypothesis, in which everything appears to be in perfect harmony, can be farther from the truth than the seemingly most improbable possibilities. From the open pages of this

> ancient work there arises a whole world, which the reader can see and hear and judge for himself.[4]

Like many others, *Njal's Saga* begins with a prologue which presents in microcosm the issues which when fully played out will constitute the final tragedy. It contains both a model solution, showing how the problems which lead to disaster in the main body of the saga could be resolved when Iceland's institutions were functioning properly, while at the same time setting in motion a complicated chain of plots and circumstances from which the protagonists' heroism and intelligence fail to extricate them.

The story opens with the planned wedding of Hrut to Unn, the daughter of Mord Fiddle, Njal's immediate predecessor as Iceland's most important legal sage: "no judgment was considered valid unless he had participated in it" (ch. 1). However, just before the ceremony is performed, Hrut leaves for Norway to claim a large inheritance left by his deceased brother. He plans to return in three years, but the evil and amorous Queen Gunnhild compels him to become her lover, and forces him to remain longer if he is to collect his money and save his life. When he finally persuades her to release him, she curses his forthcoming marriage and promises he will be unable to consummate it, thereby creating the grounds for a divorce.

Gunnhild and Norway represent two snares which appear frequently in the sagas: the perils of allowing women too much influence and the danger of seeking favor in Norway. *Njal's Saga* joins others in questioning whether the broad and exceptional legal privileges women held under the Icelandic republic were salutary. Gunnhild's selfishness foreshadows the quarrel of Gunnar's and Njal's wives which propel these best of friends to their doom. The saga's author scapegoated women as the behind-the-scenes *agents provocateurs* of the island's disastrous feuds, thereby providing the excuse required to reduce them to the submissive status more general in European Christendom. Similarly, Norway and its monarchs appear as corrupt and dishonorable in many sagas. Their favorite villain was Harald Fair-Hair (d. 930), whose consolidation of Norway into an autocratic kingdom was responsible for the great migration of his freedom-loving subjects to Iceland. The story of Gunnhild could be a sly hint that Icelanders' submission in the 1260s to their former homeland might not have been wise.[5]

Gunnhild's spell works. Upon Hrut's return, his efforts to do a husband's duty with Unn are unsuccessful. She therefore demands her legal right to a divorce and division of their property. Upon her father's advice, she is careful to declare the divorce "as correctly as possible according to the procedures of the Althing and the common law of the land" (ch. 7). When Mord demands Unn's money at the Althing, Hrut's defense emphasizes his good motives both in trying to return to Iceland on schedule and attempting to consummate the marriage, as opposed to Mord's and Unn's greed and reliance on the letter of the law rather than true justice: "You are pressing this claim with greed and aggression, not decency and fairness. These are the reasons I resist it" (ch. 8). Having convinced himself that justice is on his side, Hrut has no compunction about thrusting the law aside. He challenges the feeble Mord to single combat. Advised that "if you fight Hrut you will lose not only your money but your life," Mord backs down. The assembled people mock the erstwhile sage, who loses his reputation from this incident. As at other times in the sagas, public opinion has to judge between conflicting ideas of law and justice. In this case, instead of backing Mord, the community sides with common sense justice even where it undermines the authority of the court and legal order and is supported only by the threat of what seems to be overbearing violence against an old man. In other words, the relationship of law and justice is hopelessly ambiguous even at the start of *Njal's Saga*, symbolically the beginning of the Icelandic republic: issues are so tangled that disputes must be solved so the outcome is unjust to someone.

However, the matter does not end there. Unn returned home with her father and "frittered away" her estate (ch. 18). When he died, she went to her kinsman Gunnar, a paragon of all the Icelandic virtues: "an outstanding warrior, courteous, fearless, generous, even-tempered, loyal to friends" (ch. 19), and asked him to revive her suit. Since his obligation to support his kin in court takes precedence over his knowledge that Unn is a greedy schemer, he agrees. Gunnar brings the case to Njal, whose "skill in the law was unequalled . . . a wise, gentle man of great integrity" (ch. 20). Njal too predicts Unn's case will be "dangerous" — its ramifications will destroy Njal and the Althing itself — but he too places loyalty to a friend and, in this case, devotion to the law itself over Hrut's ambiguous appeal to justice.

Njal's strategy is to make the legality of Hrut's challenge to Mord Fiddle the issue of the case. The dispute from Njal's perspective has gone beyond whether Unn or Hrut is right — which cannot be resolved anyway — to whether people can challenge each other to duels and thus undermine the very principle behind the Althing. So Gunnar is to disguise himself in Hrut's presence, and get him to admit that his intimidation of Mord had no legal basis. Hrut falls for the bait with the help of some liquor: "Stupid people thought it was law; whereas in reality the claim could have been revived at another Althing if he had had the courage to do it" (ch. 22). So Gunnar brings up the claim now that Mord is dead, but in his typical impatience does so before Njal arrives to provide legal advice. Hrut declares the case nullified as Gunnar neglected to obtain three witnesses to the conversation in which Hrut admitted he had a valid claim. When Njal arrives, he tells Gunnar to be patient and let him develop further legal issues, but now it is Gunnar who thinks it is only just to give Hrut a taste of his own legal medicine: "I will give you the same chance you gave my kinsman Mord Fiddle."

At this point, the Althing does its job — temporarily. Hrut's brother Hoskuld advises him to pay up, arguing that "you would have no more chance against Gunnar than Mord Fiddle would have had against you" (ch. 24). The saga's author is careful to show the equivalence of Hrut's and Gunnar's behavior, and Mord's and Njal's. Despite the rule of "law," adversaries on either side are willing to use either legal technicalities, trial by combat, or an appeal to true justice when the situation suits them. By counseling peace and offering to pay half of Unn's damages himself, Hoskuld illustrates that the Althing's real purpose was to provide a site where questions of honor, property, and even murder, in which real blame was usually impossible to discover in a morass of circumstances and counter-claims, could be compromised through financial payments. But the brothers leave the court, promising Gunnar he too will be "paid for this injustice" (ch. 24); their tone indicates they do not mean in money.

These initial proceedings establish that law and the Althing are already hanging by a thread as the saga opens. Remembering Njal's date of birth as that of the Althing's, the author is suggesting the Althing was always precarious in the face of Icelandic tempers and the competing notions of law and justice people brought to the court. Mord Fiddle's legal expertise, and thus the equation of law with its letter and legal procedure, is questioned when the community forces him to accept the *de facto* legitmacy of Hrut's challenge to trial by combat. Duelling and fighting it out to determine justice may be either a holdover from pre-

Althing days or the percolation of European aristocratic behavior, but in either case it will be resorted to, not by individuals, but by large numbers of men as *Njal's Saga* and the Icelandic republic evolve.

Njal's and Gunnar's own behavior cause us to question the legitimacy of the Althing and rule of its law as well. Njal must use unjust means (the tricking of Hrut through the disguise of Gunnar) to plead what may be *technically* a just case, although both Njal and Gunnar question the moral validity of Unn's claim. Then Gunnar, who was trying to catch Hrut on a technicality, trips up on one himself by not having witnesses present, whereupon he tries to salvage his case by resorting to the same "illegal" challenge he was trying to overcome! To sum up, there is an utter confusion of moral and legal rights, the competing validity of codes of law, and how to best enforce them. The best men — Gunnar and Njal, like Mord Fiddle — are prostituting law to family connections.

To drive home the point that a compromise which satisfies no one but gives everyone something is the only solution if keeping the peace is the goal, the saga contains another story to complement Hoskuld's conciliatory gesture. Hoskuld was not always so prudent: largely to get rid of his daughter Hallgerd — after Unn and Gunnhild the third *femme fatale* in the saga — an "impetuous and willful" girl, he forced her to marry Thorvald, an equally "stubborn and unrelenting" man (ch. 9). Hallgerd continued to be "demanding and prodigal" with her husband; Thorvald slapped her when she retorted, after they ran out of food one year, "I don't care at all if you and your father starve" (ch. 11). Upon hearing about the slap, Hallgerd's foster-father Thjostolf, a man with no regard for law whatever as he "had killed many men and paid compensation for none" (ch. 9), struck Thorvald dead.

Osvif, Thorvald's father, then sought his legal right to compensation for his son's death. After being prevented by a sorcerer from reaching Thjostolf's farm, which would surely have led to his own death, Osvif went to Hoskuld instead: "One may look for honor where honor abounds" was his argument to the well-regarded Hoskuld. This time his brother Hrut returned the favor from the Unn/Gunnar case, arbitrated the situation, and awarded Osvif a "generous" two hundred ounces of silver. Hrut threw in a fine cloak to seal the bargain, "and Osvif is now out of the saga," the author laconically notes (ch. 12). In the best of circumstances, kin recognized when one of their own had done wrong, shared responsibility, and forestalled further vengeance by arbitrating situations graciously and generously. Hrut's cloak will be remembered nostalgically when Njal's similar gift is considered an insult after tensions escalate and respect for law has totally broken down. That it was only through magic that Osvif was forestalled from meeting Thjostolf and almost certain death once again suggests a precarious legal system only held together by men like Hrut and Hoskuld who can swallow their pride and hold their tempers.

Thjostolf strikes again, literally, when he kills Hallgerd's second husband whom she has once again provoked into striking her. Hrut and Hoskuld give the man's brother generous gifts even though Hrut kills Thjostolf himself, and therefore they are not legally obligated to pay compensation: ''People will praise us if we give him gifts, and he would be our friend for life,'' Hrut argues (ch. 19). Where there is a genuine desire to heal rather than prolong feuds, the saga suggests, cases need not even reach the Althing. Doing justice as perceived by the community earned landowners respect and good followings, which paradoxically then came in useful at the Althing, where powerful litigants had to appear with armed supporters to counter their adversaries who would do likewise. Thus, even while Hrut and Hoskuld appear to be doing justice for its own sake, they are forced to have ulterior motives: reputation for just behavior and acquiring followers was a prerequisite of even having a chance at justice once the legal system came into play.

The fortunate solutions achieved by Hrut and Hoskuld with Hallgerd's first two husbands does not work for her third, who is none other than Gunnar. He had sailed to Norway, where he won great reknown for his fighting and raiding. Njal considers this a mixed blessing: ''Many will envy you and force you to defend yourself often'' (ch. 32), once again hinting that Icelanders seeking gold and glory in Norway only ensnare themselves. Upon his return Gunnar marries Hallgerd, whose great beauty triumphs over multiple warnings from both Njal and her uncle Hrut. The alternating feasts Njal and Gunnar host for each other, symbolically the symbiotic relationship of Iceland's law and spirit, become excuses for Hallgerd to quarrel with Njal's strong-willed wife Bergthora. A chain of murders begins when Hallgerd has a servant of Njal's killed while he is cutting timber on land the men own jointly. Bergthora then orders the murderer killed, and the situation escalates up the social ladder to the point where Njal's sons avenge the murder of Thord Freedmansson, their foster-father, by Gunnar's foreman, Byrnjolf the Unruly. Compensation rises from twelve to two hundred ounces of silver according to the status of the victims. Despite their spouses' efforts to goad them to hostility, Njal's and Gunnar's friendship holds. "As in many cases where tempers are provoked, there are two sides to every question where vengeance is sought" (ch. 44), notes Njal. This might be *the* message of the saga, and articulates its quest to find a legal system that satisfies a sense of justice while containing tempers and vengeance.

It is Bergthora, "an exceptional and courageous, if a little harsh, woman" (ch. 20), who once again achieves a precarious peace. Gunnar runs out of food during a famine because he has too generously aided his starving countrymen. An evil man named Otkel refuses to sell to him from his surplus, although he unloads a worthless slave named Melkolf on the unsuspecting Gunnar. At this point, as Njal laments his friend's plight, Bergthora speaks up: "Why do you talk so much about it? Give Gunnar the hay and food he needs, since you have plenty." Why Njal had not already done so can only be explained by the wives' hostility, which it was the men's responsibility to end. Upon delivering the provisions, Njal tells Gunnar to "turn to me and never to anyone else when you find yourself in need" (ch. 47). Order has been restored through Bergthora's *manly* action, for she has made the peace after her son Skarp-Hedin refused to commit yet another murder at her bequest with the words "We are not women, flying into a rage at every little thing" (ch. 44).

The complicated gender issues involved in the feud between Njal and Gunnar are underlined by a short, and apparently irrelevant, anecdote which precedes it. At Gunnar's wedding, his uncle Thrain Sigfusson divorced his wife Thorhild the Poetess when she spontaneously criticized him in verse for ogling Thorgerd, Hallgerd's fourteen-year-old daughter by a former marriage. Thrain not only rebuked her "obscene sarcasm," but divorced her on the spot, turned her out of the feast, and arranged his instantaneous betrothal to the girl (ch. 34)! It is difficult to know what to make of this story — did the saga writer intend to say men could have controlled their wives if only they had the nerve, thereby stopping the feuding they caused? Is Thrain a model for Njal and Gunnar? Or is his conduct a cure that is worse than the disease — men had the power to ride roughshod over women's rights, but then what would have happened to the great, strong-minded women like Bergthora who were so integral to Icelandic society? Thorhild is a poet Thrain would silence and replace with a pretty child. To have a Bergthora, you had to risk a Hallgerd. Thorhild, who is being ignored, may symbolize too the Icelandic literary tradition which represents the voice of justice. One could imagine the arguments that developed over this part of the saga on those Icelandic nights, and women's active participation in them.

No sooner does Bergthora restore peace than Hallgerd initiates the quarrel which leads to Gunnar's death. She instructs the slave Melkolf to steal food from his former master Otkel, and then set fire to the storeroom to disguise the theft. Otkel and his friends learn the true culprit, and summon Gunnar to the Althing in an insulting manner. Otkel turns down Gunnar's offer of double compensation for his losses even though he had foisted off the responsible scoundrel on him in the first place — he wants Gunnar's humiliation, not his money. But Otkel changes his tune when a rumor — which may or may not be true, the saga does not say — circulates that Gunnar is planning another challenge of single combat against Gizur the White, the most prominent individual behind Otkel's scheme. Gizur is terrified, and his response indicates that Gunnar's technically illegal challenge may do Iceland a lot of good. He not only persuades Otkel to back down and offer Gunnar any settlement he wishes, but becomes a force for good in the rest of the saga, bringing Christianity to Iceland, prosecuting the burners of Njal's house, and helping to restore order if not law after the final battle. But now it is Gunnar who is enraged and determined to humiliate Otkel. Njal talks him into agreeing to settle, but his terms are every bit as humiliating to Otkel and his supporters as was Otkel's refusal of his earlier offer. He awards Otkel the treacherous slave who set fire to his stores and then demands compensation for himself as Otkel hid Melkolf's true character when he sold him. Even so, Otkel and his people are willing to agree if Gunnar and Otkel swear friendship. "Never, as long as I live" (ch. 51) is Gunnar's response.

Gunnar will not live long. He will perish for the same reason as the Icelandic republic. He is too proud to compromise, forgive, or realize that the justice of the case has become an issue far greater than the personal injury done to him, that reconciliation is the only outcome that will keep the peace and do justice to the community and the many people now entangled on either side of a complicated dispute. Yet has he done wrong in refusing to compromise? Njal will also die soon even though he compromises in every conceivable situation, suggesting the Icelandic republic had reached the point of no return.

Even if self-government in Iceland still had a chance, Otkel and Gunnar ensure that it disappears. Otkel "accidentally," the saga says in what may be an ironic statement given its high improbability, rides his horse into Gunnar when he is sowing grain. Further insults goad Gunnar into killing Otkel and some of his friends. He is prosecuted at the Althing, where he is taunted by the prosecutor: "Will you challenge me to single combat, as usual, and refuse to obey the law?" Gunnar has gone beyond challenging individuals: in his rage that he is being tried for killing an evil man who obviously provoked him, he claims to have declared Otkel an outlaw for riding him down, thereby earning the right to kill him, and imposes a "lawful, binding, and absolute interdict" — which is absurd — on the whole proceeding against himself. In fact, he demands the prosecutor be outlawed for taking the case to the Althing! Gunnar is clearly out of his mind: his insistence on ideal justice has blinded him to the reality that justice needs a context in which it can be enforced. As Gunnar demands that he, not the Althing, be taken as the arbiter of justice, Njal saves the day, remarking with true justice that "there is much to be said for both sides of the case" (ch. 56). Njal and Gunnar are still together, although barely, and their compensation to Otkel's family once again restores peace. But by insisting that his standard of absolute right be accepted as law, Gunnar is in fact hastening the law's imminent destruction.

Gunnar's arrogance and reputation provoke other men to bait him. Again he is technically the victim. The families of Starkad and Egil Kolsson, "arrogant, brutal men who trampled on the rights of others" (chs. 57-58) try to knock Gunnar down instead of his horse during one of the horse-fights the Icelanders frequently staged. (In these horse fights, men stood behind horses with goads so they stood on their hind legs and attacked each other.) Gunnar kills them when they ambush him. Another complicated lawsuit ensues in which Gunnar's plea of self-defense wins. "The law is on your side," remarks Mord Valgardsson, who prosecuted Gunnar and was the hidden hand behind many of the plots against him. "But we find it hard to put up with," he adds, speaking for a community that is being continuously disrupted by Gunnar's feuds and people taking the law into their own hands. A second ambush is planned, but Njal learns of it, warns Gunnar, and somehow manages another reconciliation. Then a third group sets off against Gunnar. He kills them, and once again the jury "without hesitation all found for Gunnar" (ch. 74). Nevertheless, Gunnar was required to pay compensation for the dead men to their kin; with his brother Kolskegg, who fought valiantly at his side, he was outlawed for three years. Although declared innocent, Gunnar suffers the punishment the guilty would usually have in this situation. His very presence threatens community survival.

The turning point of the saga occurs as Gunnar prepares to go into exile, with Njal's warning of more "trouble once you return" (ch. 76) ringing in his ears. Gunnar rides away; his horse stumbles, and he catches a glimpse of his farm: "How beautiful are the slopes, more beautiful than they have ever been before, the golden cornfields and freshly-mown hay. I am going home, and will never go away" (ch. 76). This brief passage, the only paean to nature in any major saga, affirms Gunnar's love for and identification with Iceland. His proud, unconquerable spirit is the nation's essence, his indefinable, romantic love for the land a truer expression of Iceland than laws and courts. Worn out with threats, taunts, and attacks, Gunnar would rather die than betray his heroic nature and the republic it embodies. He would rather perish in combat than slink away, as from his perspective thirteenth-century Iceland certainly would have by doing homage to Norway and Rome. The law's (Njal's) best friend had to be out-lawed by a society which had betrayed justice, and then be martyred that the memory of Iceland at its greatest survive. Gunnar goes home, where he is massacred when his wife Hallgerd, reminding him of a time when he, too, had slapped her, refuses to lend him strands of her hair to repair his bowstring. He kills two men and wounds eight before dying, for the attackers, to their credit and Iceland's, still have the decency to fight fairly. Gizur the White rejects Mord's suggestion that they could have saved these lives by burning down the house: "Never, even if it cost me my own life" (ch. 76) Gizur replies. He also orders that there be no pillaging. Some vestiges of honor remain among Gunnar's foes, reinforcing the moral ambiguity that serves as a subtext to a reading that would only take Gunnar's perspective.

Gunnar's death so disturbs Njal that even he begins to modify his stance as the peacemaker: he recommends that his kinsmen kill only a few of the murderers in revenge, probably realizing they could not restrain themselves entirely in any case. If Njal must abandon law to do justice, what hope is there for anyone else? Gunnar's ghost rises from its grave, "towering like an oak in the forest of battle," reiterating his credo that he would "rather die than surrender." "This was his message for us," ominously remarks Skarp-Hedin, the most warlike of Njal's sons, whose own hot temper accelerates what is fast becoming his father's, and the republic's, inevitable doom (ch. 78). We might also argue, although an alternative case could be made, that Gunnar's spirit is being invoked by the saga's author to rebuke an Iceland that preferred domination by Norway to republican instability and freedom.

Two solutions appear to Iceland's problems between the death of its spirit — Gunnar — and the final demise of its decaying legal system — Njal. Depending on how the saga is interpreted, they are either welcome replacements for an ungovernable nation, pathetic alternatives to a heroic one, or the only straws remaining for a drowning social order to grasp. One possibility appears symbolically through the story of Gunnar's brother Kolskegg, who accepts becoming a non-Icelander as his fate. Under the terms of his outlawry, he first goes to Norway, then to Denmark, then to Russia, and finally to Constantinople, where, like many Scandinavians and Icelanders, he joined the Byzantine Emperor's Varangian Guard. But his frequent moves suggest the true Icelander could never be comfortable in the monarchies which ruled most of the world.

Kolskegg also embraces Christianity, which for Icelanders is connected intimately with the Norwegian monarchy. Thangbrand, an emissary of the proselytizing King Olaf, who also converted Norway, first preaches the gospel on the island. However, he is ill-treated, and returns to Norway with such tales of woe that Olaf threatens to put to death all the Icelanders visiting his country at the time. But Gizur the White, who is one of them, dissuades him, and offers to preach the faith to his compatriots. Christianity thus makes its appearance in Iceland not bringing peace but discord: at the next Althing both Christians and pagans "renounced their allegiance to the laws." "At the Law Rock, things were in such turmoil that nobody could make himself heard," and "the situation was very ugly." Only the dramatic conversion of Thorgeir, one of the most respected pagan priests, saves the day. His argument for the new religion is purely practical and nationalistic: "Life becomes impossible if we do not all have the same law. If the laws are divided the peace will be sundered, and that is intolerable" (ch. 105). Although the pagans felt "incredibly betrayed," they agreed to abandon the old Norse faith. The Icelanders were willing to surrender their religion in the interests of preserving the peace, but time soon tells that they are less able to give up their personal vendettas.[6]

In fact, the first episode in *Njal's Saga* to follow the mass conversion drives home this point. Once Christianity has come, there are two laws anyway — Christian and Althing justice. Njal's son Hoskuld had been killed by Thrain Sigfusson's brother-in-law Lytig to avenge the murder of Thrain during the Bergthora-Hallgerd feud. Amundi the Blind, Njal's grandson, demands monetary compensation from Lytig for his father's death at the Althing. Lytig refuses since he had already paid Njal. Amundi then challenges Icelandic law in the name of Christian justice: "How can this be just and right before God! If I were blessed with sight, I would be fully compensated for my father or take blood-vengeance. May God judge between us" (ch. 106)! God apparently does: Amundi's eyes open for a moment, which enables him to slay Lytig before his blindness is restored. The first fruits of a typical Christian miracle are used to revive a blood feud already resolved, at least from the perspective of old Icelandic law. Alternatively, they may be regarded as enabling a truer justice to be accomplished where the earlier system had compromised with iniquity. The saga writer straddles the issue.

Njal is again the peacemaker. He tells Amundi: "You cannot be blamed for what you did. This warns others never to rebuff those who are so closely related" who ask compensation for murdered kin (ch. 106). Still, only half the usual compensation goes to Lytig's family, emphasizing the impossibility of pinpointing blame or justice in this case.

Christianity does nothing to stop the deterioration of Icelandic society. Njal had been fostering Thrain Sigfusson's son Hoskuld as part of the settlement between their families: a son of the enemy clan, of the same name, replaced Njal's own slain son. Perhaps that was why Njal came to love him more than his own children; additionally, Hoskuld resembles Njal: "soft-spoken and generous, a calm man yet very skilled with arms, he never spoke ill of anyone" (ch. 94). Njal arranges his marriage to Hildigunn, the beautiful but "harsh and ruthless" (ch. 95) daughter of Flosi, a powerful chieftain. When she refuses the match because her bridegroom is not one of Iceland's thirty-six chieftains, Njal persuades the Althing to add a fifth, appellate court, to the four existing Quarter Courts, then three new chieftainships, one of which Hoskuld will hold. This may seem like nepotism, especially given the arm-twisting Njal employs to get his way. But Njal plausibly presents the new court as a last-ditch effort to save the Althing and the republic. People had stopped advancing lawsuits because juries corrupted by both parties could not agree on decisions, and "since no one made any progress with legal actions, they preferred to settle their claims with weapons" (ch. 97). The new court would be the final court of appeals where other juries could not reach the required unanimous verdicts or if procedural irregularities arose. Hoskuld, a surrogate Njal who is also a priest, that is, a symbolic representation of the old Icelandic legal system with the leavening of a spirit of Christian charity, is given a chance to restore order through reformed institutions. The author of the saga cleverly fuses Njal's story with the historical fact of the Fifth Court's establishment in the early eleventh century to drive home his message that the legal system was beyond repair.

The futility of Njal's machinations soon appears. His elevation of Hoskuld infuriates his own sons. Mord Valgardsson plays upon their jealousy, and insinuates that Hoskuld is secretly plotting to kill them; they pre-emptively murder their saintly foster-brother instead. Njal has become irrelevant, as he realizes: ''I was seldom left out when their plans were good''(ch. 110), he complains to Bergthora, and predicts the death of his entire family as a result — symbolically, the end of traditional law and its defenders. The younger generation has deserted the republic established by their forefathers and replaced it with personal vengeance. But a plausible subtext is that Njal's favoritism, the corruption of the law by influential chiefs and the denial of real justice, prompts both Amundi and Njal's sons to seek their rightful due.

Similar pressures are felt in Hoskuld's family. His father-in-law Flosi is willing to settle honorably with Njal's clan: ''I shall press your claims to the limit of the law, or else conclude a settlement which will satisfy all good men and the demands of honor'' (ch. 116), he informs Hoskuld's widow Hildigunn. But she hurls at him the cloak he gave Hoskuld, covered with blood, and calls on absolute Christian justice to override the compromise demanded by republican Icelandic law: ''I call upon God and all good men to witness that I demand of you in the name of Christ and of your courage and manhood, to avenge every wound in his body, or become an object of contempt to all men'' (ch. 116). Flosi throws the cloak back at her, damning her as a ''Monster!'' His face rapidly changes color from blood-red to pale-green to deathly black. He consults with Hoskuld's uncles: Ketil is willing to reconcile, but the other two demand *both* outlawry and blood-vengeance (ch. 117) for Njal's sons, two utterly incompatible punishments as Flosi points out. As Flosi goes to the Althing, he is under nearly unendurable pressure from his own family, as Njal had earlier been with respect to Hoskuld. Their kinsmen are demanding violent solutions which may achieve justice but which will wreck the jerry-rigged system of Althing and courts which the great chiefs had crafted to prevent the bloodbaths for which their households were lusting.

Suspense builds as Flosi and Njal both appear at the Althing. Each recruits an unprecedented body of supporters. However, Njal's impetuous son, Skarp-Hedin, reduces his father's strength through insulting important people by reminding them of their cowardice in failing to take blood-vengeance for murdered relatives. The Althing is being mocked within its own precincts. Skarp-Hedin even threatens to murder the powerful Thorkel Braggart when Thorkel mockingly terms him more fit to pick mare's dung from his teeth than to stand up against injustice like a man (ch. 120).

Despite his son's efforts to provoke a battle, Njal makes one last, hopeless effort. He pleads, "I loved Hoskuld more than my own sons; when I learned he had been killed, the sweetest light of my eyes was put out" (ch. 122). This is understandable — the survival of men like Hoskuld in the new generation represent the only hope for the continued rule of law. Njal and Flosi persuade Hoskuld's kin to accept the unprecedented compensation of six hundred ounces of silver. All of Njal's supporters contribute, recognizing that a family feud has escalated into a question of communal survival. As had another Hoskuld in the prologue to the saga, Njal attempts to seal the bargain with a gesture of good will by placing an elegant silk cloak and pair of boots on top of the silver. But perhaps thinking of the cloak Hildigunn had flung at him when she attacked his masculinity in failing to take revenge, Flosi regards Njal's friendly gesture as a sign of contempt. He turns the tables on Njal and questions his manhood as Njal could never grow a beard. This prompts Skarp-Hedin to taunt that Flosi was serving as a male troll's lover. Flosi promises never to touch the money, and Skarp-Hedin is exultant: "They now have no legal grounds for prosecuting us," he tells Njal. Ironically, the very man who had in effect denounced the Althing's way of settling disputes pretends that it is still functioning. It is Njal who brings him up short — "Then disaster will fall on us all" (ch. 123) — for he realizes Flosi has now abandoned a solution through the courts. Given the saga's misogyny, it is logical that the final disaster is heralded by the figurative transformation of men into women, whose malice is blamed for much of the trouble. A subtext may be that the old Icelandic rules had in fact been cowardly, womanly, and in need of purging. A second subtext may be that the sexual criticisms masked the need of Icelanders to attain a psychological sense of worth, or manhood, in some form of combat which the Althing existed to thwart. At any rate, when the greatest financial settlement in Icelandic history can be spurned, the obsolescence of the Althing is sealed.

Flosi gathers his forces to attack Njal — after praying and attending Mass, which again underlines the ambiguous relationship of Christianity to Icelandic law and justice. Njal has ample warning but is sure he can win the day if his family only remains in their house which serves as a fortress. "It was hard to overcome Gunnar even though he stood alone against many" when he remained indoors, Njal remarks, still trusting to the honor of Icelanders. Skarp-Hedin, who stands for a new Iceland, knows better: "The chieftains who attacked Gunnar were men of honor who would rather have retreated than burn him in his house. But these people will resort to fire if they cannot destroy us otherwise." Njal persists: "You plan to override my advice and be disrespectful, and not for the first time. When you were younger and listened to me, things went better for you" (ch. 128).

Njal is not only speaking about the immediate peril. The dialogue with Skarp-Hedin is a meditation on the system of law Njal represents. By refusing to stand outside his house, Njal is performing a symbolically equivalent action to Gunnar's refusal to leave his fields. Neither will forsake the Iceland he loves. By remaining in the house and insisting that even an attack following the breakdown of law be conducted in an honorable manner — although he knows it will not — Njal "would rather die than surrender" as Gunnar's ghost had proclaimed. Njal says that in earlier times his sons, that is the heirs of Iceland's institutions, would have obeyed the law of their fathers, and it served them well. But now it is the sons who are right: by staying within the house, the law, they are in fact doomed. Njal does succeed in shaming his sons into doing his will, but as Skarp-Hedin realizes: "His fate is sealed now. But I will please my father by burning up in the house with him, for I am not afraid to die." The incident would have told men of the thirteenth century that their republic had to die, law had become irrelevant, but those who tried to remain within the house of Njal should be honored for a special Icelandic heroism — defense of law, not martial combat.

Flosi has a parallel dilemma, as he did at the Althing. Once more, the difference between him and Njal is that he is goaded successfully into doing what he knows to be wrong. Njal shows us a good man cannot survive honorably in this wreck of a society; Flosi shows us he can by ceasing to be good and making survival rather than justice the supreme test of moral decisions. Flosi's people first assault Njal's house and are being cut down. Flosi realizes there are only two choices: give up the attack, in which case Njal's sons would surely mount an attack against him, or "set fire to the house and burn them alive, which is a grave sin before God, as we are Christians" (ch. 128).

One person escapes the conflagration: Kari of Orkney, who had once rescued Njal's sons from the pursuing forces of Earl Hakon of Norway on one of their overseas journeys. At the time, he was visiting Njal with his twelve-year-old son Thord, whom Njal had adopted as a foster-son. The brave boy insists on remaining with Njal and Bergthora, who lie down in their bed and prepare to die. But Skarp-Hedin hoists Kari through a hole in the ceiling just before the roof collapses, with instructions to take revenge: "I shall laugh, brother-in-law, if you escape, for you will avenge us all" (ch. 129). Here is the voice of vengeance rejoicing that this code of justice will continue, even after his own death. But Flosi finds no joy in the victory: "This burning will lead to many of our deaths and others will lose all their wealth" (ch. 130).

Headed by Gizur the White, Njal's friends and kinsmen insist that Mord Valgardsson take over the prosecution of the burners. Mord has a great reputation for legal acumen, but he only uses the law for personal advantage and evil schemes. He represents a different but equally real deterioration in the character of the republic from Njal's generation. He secretly had encouraged the burning, and only agrees to prosecute when his wife threatens to divorce him for not doing his duty. While the case is being prepared, Kari makes an attempt to kill Flosi, who forbids revenge when the attack fails: "We have pushed him beyond endurance, and he only acted in accordance with his duty, and he is no coward" (ch. 136). Instead, Flosi predicts, "we shall fight this out in earnest" at the Althing. Given the tense atmosphere, it is even ambiguous whether Flosi's use of "fight" is ambiguous — is there even a question whether the Althing will deteriorate into a pitched battle, or is he still hoping the law can reassert itself?

Flosi hires a famous lawyer named Eyjolf to handle the case. Eyjolf is yet another symbol of the law's deterioration after Njal — he only agrees to become involved after being illegally bribed with a valuable bracelet. Flosi must also show up in court with a large number of men and stay continually alert for possible attempts on his life, because of the great outrage over Njal's murder. The case is tried in the Fifth Court, the new tribunal established by Njal whose very existence was the first step leading to this chain of events.

A complicated series of legal maneuvers ensues between two lawyers who have already been identified as hypocrites unconcerned with real justice. Eyjolf declares Mord's witnesses incompetent as some of them were either his relatives or poor people without land. Mord in turn challenges Flosi's defense and demands his outlawry, and that of Eyjolf, not for the murder of Njal, but for bribing a lawyer. The scene is depressingly reminiscent of the United States Congress's behavior in the late 1980s, when most of the members were less angry that President Reagan and his advisors had solicited private money to enable the Contras to murder people in Nicaragua and destroy a legitimate government, than that it had not been done through procedural channels with the knowledge of the legislature. Mord swears to a falsehood knowingly — that his witnesses are in fact legitimate — which everyone knows is a lie but which has to be accepted as fact for the duration of the case although it opens him up to prosecution when it has been decided. Was it for this system of law that Njal gave his life? Both sides use all the legal talent they can find and consult with many wise men — the author is careful to ensure that all of Iceland participates in this travesty and that the corrupt lawyers are true representatives of the general consensus. After a seemingly interminable — another sign justice is being flouted — suspense-filled pleading of technicalities, in which each side tries to argue the other has no legal case instead of dealing with the problem of murder and social disorder, Eyjolf and Flosi "win": Mord has forgotten to disqualify six of the forty-two judges as required, and so loses the case. Given his reluctance to plead and his secret role in encouraging the burners, perhaps Mord's error was intentional — a point the saga leaves open. The upshot of this case is to fill the reader with revulsion at the court's inability to do justice, and outrage that the burners cannot be lawfully punished. But in being led to believe they ought to have their just deserts, outside the law, we too have become complicitous in the destruction of the Icelandic republic, symbolized by the burning of Njal.

As Flosi predicts, the Althing turns from a court into a battleground. Eyjolf is killed, and Flosi and his followers are forced to flee. But following the carnage, most of the chiefs and retainers reconvene. All are willing to make peace except Kari, the symbolic survivor from the house of law. Is the saga telling us he is now the voice of justice rather than of those who would continue the system of payments and compromises, or are we presented with yet another irresolvable ambiguity? Another unprecedented compensation, eight hundred ounces of silver — the monetary stakes have escalated in tandem with the social cost of violence and disorder from the saga's beginning — is paid to the great chief Hall of Sida for the loss of his son. Ironically, but deliberately, Hall is rewarded after having offered to forego any compensation if only the contending parties agree to restore peace. Possible moral number one: the disinterested peacemaker receives the greatest reward. Possible moral number two: there is no peace, a surrogate Njal is now useless, Althing justice has ended.

Flosi and the burners have three years to leave Iceland. In one of the few poems or songs inserted in the saga, Kari sends them off with these words: "Men have joked about the burning of Njal and his sons. But they do wrong, and when this Althing ends, they will be grunting a different tune in Svinafell" (ch. 138). Read symbolically, Kari warns us that we ought not to mock the end of traditional Iceland. Svinafell, the home of Flosi's family and the source of *Njal's Saga*, will now be "grunting." These words not only signify Kari's unslaked thirst for vengeance but contain a powerful, hidden meaning which could probably not be articulated openly around Flosi's descendants or in an Iceland subjected to Norway: that what replaces the Althing will be less noble — either chaos, submission to Norway, or domination by the church. Instead of free men trying to work out their problems according to law and reason, "grunting" will be heard before authority.

Kari massacres most of the remaining burners before they have a chance to take up their outlawries. Another fifteen are killed in a battle for the Irish throne — Icelanders who are not killing themselves at home are dying in the service of foreign kings. But Flosi neither takes Kari to court nor tries to revenge himself even though he has the opportunity. In fact, when Kari is in Orkney for the purpose of killing Flosi, Flosi saves Kari's life. Kari could not restrain himself and burst in on a feast held by the Earl where one Gunnar Lambason was condemning Njal for cowardice by remaining in the house to be burned. Kari rushed in and killed Gunnar, but Flosi successfully pleaded to the Earl that "he only did what was his duty" (ch. 155). Flosi thus becomes the symbol of a new social order based on Christian love and forgiveness. This must have pleased his powerful heirs who first heard *Njal's Saga*, for it rehabilitated their ancestor as the initiator of a less corrupt, more decent society.[7]

Was this really the case? Flosi and Kari both undertake pilgrimages to Rome. Flosi pays a great deal of money to receive absolution from the Pope, perhaps a sly hint that justice was still for sale in the Christian order. He then returns to Iceland by way of Norway after receiving a gift of flour from its king. Since such shipments of food to famine-plagued Iceland were part of the conditions for submission to Norway in 1262, Flosi's journey symbolically sets the seal on Iceland's dependence on the papacy and the Norwegian crown. This may be variously interpreted as deliverance, tragedy, or curse. Kari, too, makes a pilgrimage to Rome, but his boat is shipwrecked near Flosi's estate. Determined to put his adversary's "honor to the test" (ch. 159), Kari goes to Flosi for sanctuary. Flosi shares his high-seat with Kari, and gives him the shrewish Hildigunn, widow of Hoskuld the priest, to marry. Under Flosi's benign aegis, the old Icelandic world of vengeance and "eye for an eye" justice represented by Flosi will be domesticated, along with the malicious, provocative women who characterized it.

But the saga never leaves us with solutions, only with insoluble problems. Just before the final reconciliation, one of those seemingly irrelevant anecdotes is placed. Earlier in the saga such incidents showed alternative solutions to those problems of order and justice which the saga could not solve. Now, with the problems apparently solved, a terrifying alternative appears. An Irishman has a vision. It is Good Friday, and nearly all of the many Icelanders who take part in a battle for the throne of Ireland are slain. The twelve Valkyries abandon their horses and take up the guise of domesticated women. (Is Hildigunn wearing a similar mask?) They begin to spin. But they are fashioning war and destruction, not the domestic peace that seems to be in preparation. Men's heads and intestines, swords and arrows form their deadly spinning wheels. They sing: "It is horrible to see, as blood-red clouds darken the sky, how the heavens are stained with the blood of men as the Valkyries sing their song. Let he who listens to our song learn it well and spread it to others. Let us ride our horses hard on bare backs, with swords unsheathed, away from here."

Their destination is Iceland. A "priest seemed to see a bottomless pit of ocean beside the altar, filled with terrible visions, and could not sing Mass for a long time." At Flosi's seat, "blood rained on the priest's robe on Good Friday, and he had to remove it" (ch. 157). The Valkyries still ride, they can do their evil deeds on Good Friday, their magic can stop Christianity dead in its tracks. Is the saga telling not just

Icelandic Christians, but all of us, that social harmony is always precarious, and that we will always have to resist the Valkyries who lure us into battle both at home or in distant lands? Or is their final ride a last, powerful glimpse at a lost heroic world? Or is it both?

Yet one more ambiguity ends the saga. ''People say'' this is how Flosi died, although no one really knows. He sailed to Norway as an old man to bring back timber — the other necessity on which Iceland depended from its new mother country — to build a house. Although ''people told him his ship was not seaworthy, Flosi replied that it sufficed for a doomed old man. He boarded the ship and sailed out to sea. Nothing was ever heard from him again'' (ch. 159). Is the message that someone who burns the house of justice, Njal's house, cannot build another? Flosi knows he will die; is his death telling us that Icelandic dependency on Norway is sufficient — for a doomed old society? Since the great medieval sagas, Iceland has been peaceful. But its greatness still rests in the sagas and the memories they conjure of Njal's house, Gunnar's fields, and the sky-piercing cries of the Valkyries. The fate of the Althing and Icelandic republic, destroying themselves through violence and corruption, forced to endure foreign political and ecclesiastical domination to survive in an era of chaos and economic scarcity, the too vehement pursuit of justice by some, the manipulation of law against justice by others, will stand forever in the moving pages of *Njal's Saga* as warnings to all future republics in human history.

Chapter Three

THE GREAT OUTLAW: *GRETTIR'S SAGA*

Synopsis: Grettir is an immensely strong, quarrelsome man. Paradoxically he is outlawed for a good deed's accidental consequences — he is mistaken for a troll, attacked, and slays two Icelanders in a fight in Norway. The victims' father arranges an unjust outlawry. Grettir ignores it and stays alive almost twenty years, performing many good deeds and growing morally. Yet he is repeatedly betrayed by ''respectable'' folk whose fear of Grettir's enemies outweighs their sense of gratitude or justice. He is ultimately slain through sorcery and vindicated after his death.

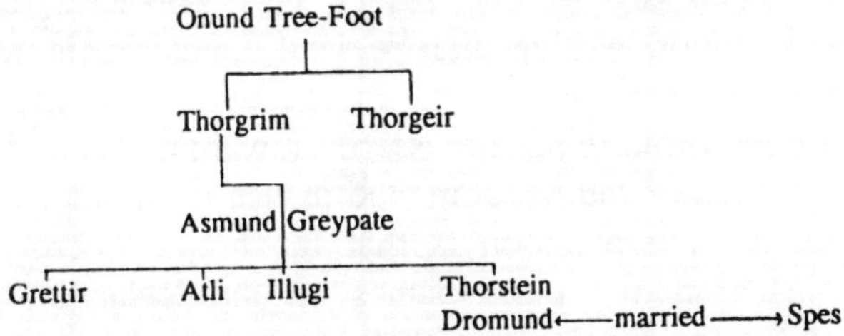

In *Grettir's Saga*, the titanic passions which both established and ruined the medieval Icelandic republic stand forth with exceptional boldness. Grettir's tragic life raises questions concerning the ability of law to govern people, and which of the available codes — pagan, Christian, blood-vengeance, the compensations paid at the Things, or community consensus — works best to do justice and to keep the peace. Through understanding the interaction of characters and events, the auditors or readers are invited to render judgments. Alas, there are no clear choices or definitive answers for Grettir, for Iceland, or for the troubled world whose dilemmas the saga will always dramatize. Peace only seems possible if we abandon the burden of trying to be free and ethical people living in a society with similar goals, and seek order without justice in the authoritarian orders of church and state, represented at the end of *Grettir's Saga* by Rome and Constantinople.

Grettir's Saga, like *Gisli's Saga*, differs from the other Icelandic epics because its hero lives nearly his entire adult life as an outlaw, the last nineteen of his forty-five years (ch. 84). No matter how obnoxious or anti-social Hrafnkel or Egil may be, they live in society and attain high status. Although by no means a totally sympathetic character, Grettir is ironically ostracized when his well-intentioned deeds have disastrous consequences, rather than for his early selfish acts which he is in the process of morally overcoming. When he gains temporary acceptance from different people while he is outside the law, it is under false identities and pretenses. Pagan ghosts remain in the land after its formal acceptance of Christianity and are evoked by old Norse curses to destroy him; his good Christian deeds are no protection against them. The outlaw Grettir attracts more and more respect and sympathy as his good deeds mount, but the Icelanders have settled down. They do not wish to jeopardize their safety by violating the law and risking retribution for harboring him even though almost everyone considers Grettir's punishment excessive. The reader may conclude that the saga's anonymous author, writing after Iceland's experiment with republican self-government had ended, has chosen to present life as tragic and absurd, where virtue is not necessarily rewarded, peace is purchased at the price of dignity and freedom, and justice is an indecipherable riddle. An alternative interpretation is that the heroic Grettir, immortalized through his saga and place names on the Icelandic landscape, has triumphed posthumously, and that heroism and virtue are sufficient compensation for those who practice them.

Like many of the sagas, Grettir's opens with a lengthy prologue which at first glance has little, though on further reflection much, to do with the story. Chapters One through Thirteen are the saga of Grettir's great-grandfather Onund Tree-Foot, so-called because he lost the lower part of a leg in a fight with a berserk named Thorir. Thorir supported King Harald Fair-Hair of Norway's successful attempt to conquer that entire nation and reduce its great free landholders to vassals. Onund, like many, chose outlawry and flight to Iceland rather than submission. His resistance introduces a main point of the saga: heroic violation of law in a tyrannical society is admirable, and constitutes the founding myth of a free society — we need only think of the Boston Tea Party. But once a self-governing nation is established, the deeds which it memorializes are now threats to order. Grettir cannot follow in Onund's footsteps and remain within the republic's laws.

Onund's tale precedes Grettir's because it is the comparable story of a similar personality in which everything works out justly and fortunately for its hero. ' Onund thus symbolizes the golden age of Iceland's founding, in which the saga-writers liked to imagine there was prosperity, justice, and plenty of room for men to be heroes. Grettir will therefore stand for the impossibility of heroism under the declining republic, and invite meditation on whether the courts and Althing ever did justice or merely preserved the peace. Much like the German philosopher Friedrich Nietzsche argued in *The Genealogy of Morals*, the consensus of numerous cowards overwhelms the occasional hero and thus government exists.

Parallels between Grettir and his ancestor are numerous. Both have adversaries named Thorir and Audun; both triumph over berserks; both have adventures in which cliffs figure prominently — Onund defeats vikings who are pillaging in Scotland, Ireland, and Norway by luring them to the edge of cliffs where they are pelted with stones (ch. 4). Three of Grettir's main adventures involve scaling cliffs. Onund does not leave Norway immediately after Harald has defeated him, but bravely returns to revenge a kinsman whose lands the king has stolen (ch. 7). Grettir also voyages to Norway following his first outlawry; there the Icelandic outcast is transformed into the champion of justice. Onund is on different occasions termed the wisest (ch. 4) and the bravest (ch. 6) of men. "Bravery" also describes Grettir (ch. 84), and his "cleverness" is apparent from the fact he can remain an outlaw in Iceland for nineteen years without being killed. Onund has a tree-foot, but is still the "briskest" (ch. 10) of men; Grettir is undone when he is poisoned by the runes carved into a tree-trunk whose wood he is splitting (ch. 81). Onund is "exceedingly moody" (ch. 3) despite his success; Grettir is also moody, and afraid of the dark and of solitude, the two perpetual companions of an outlaw. Onund is Grettir in happier times.

Our saga's author reminds us that even around 900, when Onund came to Iceland, land was already scarce, but drifts — timber and beached whales — and fish were so plentiful that "every man had of them what he would" (chs. 9 and 11). In times of plenty, law and binding authority are superfluous; Onund is welcomed by Eirik, a rich man, and receives some of his land as a gift without title. Similarly, Grettir finds a temporary refuge on the remote island of Drangey through informal acquiescence of the neighbors, but it is literally off of Iceland.

The agreement between Onund and Eirik occurred even before the Althing was founded; during the sixty-odd years of settlement (870-930) honor among former freedom-fighters in Norway sufficed to maintain order. Onund's story also recalls that an Iceland which originally began as a refuge for men outlawed unjustly for standing up to tyranny would, once it had established formal legal mechanisms, use these to outlaw similar men. However, plenty gives way to scarcity as land and timber disappear and the waters are fished too much. "Hard times as were never seen before" (ch. 12) afflict Iceland, and accord breaks down. As long as the great founders Eirik and Onund live, the peace is maintained, but their sons quarrel. Flosi, Eirik's son, demands the return of "his" land from Thorgrim and Thorgeir, Onund's sons. When they are cutting up a beached whale, some of Flosi's henchmen, claiming it as their master's, attack and kill them (ch. 12). "It is certainly a terrible thing to tell of such quarrels" (ch. 12) proclaims the saga.

But Iceland's great men neither despaired nor permitted an ecological disaster to become a political one. By this time, the legal system had begun to function. Flosi is both outlawed and compelled to pay compensation for the victims. The first of several Law-Speakers to appear in the saga, Thorkel Moon, will be a model for his degenerate forbears much as Onund's era was for future generations. He lays down the edict that "the land be shared equally, and that each man have the drifts on his own lands" (ch. 13). By accepting customary possession as ten-tenths of the law, the Althing formalized the status quo in a fair, common-sense manner. Its wisdom in averting unrest appears if we think of the history of the Americas, where the failure of Native Americans to possess titles approved by an alien legal system has been an excuse for throwing them off the land for five centuries — the process continues in Guatemala and Brazil, at least. The prologue to *Grettir's Saga* ends with a functioning, commonly accepted, and enforceable legal system that does true justice in place. The three generations which separate Onund from Grettir, who was born about 997 and died in 1042, are then sketched quickly so the reader may note the persistence and success of the new institutions.

Grettir is then born. He is perhaps the most obnoxious child and adolescent imaginable. Aged ten, to avoid the "sissy's" work of watching his father's geese, he kills the goslings, mutilates the adults, and responds with sarcasm when criticized. His father Asmund Greypate is his next victim; when he asks Grettir to massage his back, the boy scrapes it with a carding comb. Disliking the herding of horses, he flays the skin off the back of his father's prize mare so she remains in the stables and he can stay out of the cold pastures (ch. 14). At the age of fourteen Grettir, while on his way to the Althing to represent his father, kills a man named Skeggi in a dispute over who owns a meal-sack. He blames the death on trolls — a lie which will haunt him: it is when he himself is mistaken for a troll that he gets into a brawl that leads to others' deaths and his own exile from Norway. Nevertheless, no one believes Grettir about Skeggi, and he is outlawed for three years (ch. 16).

Grettir's early escapades do not win him much sympathy, but a subtext does. What is to become of a boy who has the old viking spirit in his blood in an Iceland that has settled down to farming and domesticity? In fact, Grettir parodies himself on the voyage to Norway, insulting the crew, refusing to help with sailing or bailing water on the difficult journey. Instead, he holds the knitting for the mate's wife — if they want to turn him into a woman, he'll do it to the hilt! But when a real emergency occurs and the ship is on the verge of sinking, he takes charge and comes through heroically (ch. 17). In Norway he is just as able. He destroys the ghost of Karr the Old, who has terrified all the farmers in the vicinity, and recovers for Karr's son Thorfinn the treasure the old man had taken to his grave (ch. 18). Next he wins Karr's sword from Thorfinn — the symbolic passing of a heroic torch — by slaying a band of berserks who threaten the women on Thorfinn's estate while the men are away paying homage to the king. A possible subtext is that the Norwegian monarchy demands obedience from tyrannized subjects but cannot protect them. Grettir uses both brains and brawn to deal with the berserks. At first he pretends to befriend the marauders, but then as they enter a storeroom they intend to plunder he locks them up, and slays them one by one as they try to escape (ch. 19). Word of this deed saves Grettir's life, for he soon earns the king's wrath by slaying two of his friends. It does not matter that this occurred, in the first instance, after a fair fight into which the man provoked Grettir, or that the other fellow ambushed him. Royal justice is arbitrary and personal, which also appears in the means of Grettir's salvation through the influence of Thorfinn, yet another trusted companion of the king. It seems that royal society provides no justice or safety, which leaves open much opportunity for great deeds, whereas in peaceful, republican Iceland, to which Grettir is compelled to return (ch. 24), there is justice but no room for heroes, as they have nothing to fight against.

Thus, upon his return, Grettir finds no chance to further test his mettle: ''he grew so overbearing, he thought he could do anything'' (ch. 28). In Iceland, sports had become a domesticated equivalent of war to let off steam, but Grettir cannot scale down his spirit. He nearly kills a young man he fights in a ballgame, and breaks another man's ribs during a horsefight (ch. 29) He meets his opponents from the horsefight later in a brawl in which three people are killed, and insults the powerful Thorbjorn Oxmain, ''the strongest of men,'' whose presence is needed to cool Grettir off (ch. 30). Grettir roams disconsolately around Iceland, offering to fight any four men at once, but ''finding nowhere to try his strength'' (ch. 30).

Grettir finally gets his comeuppance from a ghost named Glam, who represents Iceland's pagan and violent heritage. Glam was a gigantic shepherd of great strength, hired by the rich landowner Thorhall, on the advice of the Law-Speaker Skapti, to protect his sheep from ghosts that were killing them. But Skapti's advice is no good. The ghost kills Glam and turns him into an even more fearsome apparition. The saga states that Glam died because ''he hated church, and was godless, mean-tempered, and surly'' — in fact, he is slain on Christmas Eve for failing to fast as was then required. Read symbolically, Grettir cannot find his equal among his contempories, who are Christians; he must go back in time to the old pagans, or rather they come forward in time in the forms of Glam and Karr to confront him. Glam is a threat to Iceland's domestic peace and farming economy, and the law represented by its speaker is unable to restrain such pagan residues. Grettir, on the other hand, slays Glam after a ferocious struggle, but just as Glam himself was undone by a ghost, so is Grettir. Glam places an effective pagan curse on his adversary; Grettir would never become any stronger, would be afraid of the dark and of being alone, and would suffer perpetual bad luck: ''Until now you have won fame by great deeds, but from now only evil and manslaughter will fall on you.'' He would be condemned to dwell alone as an outlaw and yet ''find it hard to be alone — and that will drag you to your death'' (ch. 35). Ironically, just before the good deed of killing Glam starts him down the path to ruin, Grettir had made peace with his childhood sports rival, Audun (ch. 34). Grettir is cursed and punished only when it seems he is becoming unselfish and civilized. Is that because he is thereby acting against his nature — or is he the paradigm for an Iceland that loses its greatness when it becomes reduced to a nation of peaceful farmers?

Glam's curse also suggests a psychological interpretation. Grettir from childhood had freely insulted people, yet craved their appreciation of his great deeds. He therefore sought affection and recognition behind his sarcastic exterior, probably because his father had never loved him and provoked his outbursts — he was assigned menial chores and given poor clothing to wear (ch. 14). When he was treated with respect and decency, he in fact performed heroically. The saga is perhaps obliquely telling us that when people do not have worthy tasks to perform, they become small, petulant, and frustrated. We can again point to Nietzsche's *Genealogy of Morals* for a discussion of how a heroic, aristocratic age identifies its own group as "good" and opponents as "bad," without the envy and resentment of the good and strong characteristic of the "slave morality" of peaceful, republican societies.

Another way to look at Glam's curse is to take a pagan/Christian perspective. Grettir will never be stronger once he starts doing the communal will; similarly, a Christian Iceland will never be stronger than it had been before. The irreligious Glam's curse is quite effective, for under Christianity — which came to Iceland in 1000 A.D., about twenty years before Glam's curse — the violent tempers of the people do not abate, but are turned inward on themselves as they quarrel over increasingly scarce resources like too many rats in a small cage. Raiding throughout Europe, fighting against kings in Norway, serving in the Byzantine Emperor's guard, Icelanders are heroes; at home, they have the choice of petulant internal war or monotonous sheep-herding.

Grettir wastes no time leaving Iceland for Norway to escape the curse. He does a good if violent deed on the voyage over by killing one Thorbjorn Tardy who was mocking him. The crew's response is significant: Thorbjorn deserved death because he was "quarrelsome and spiteful" — traits easily developed in peaceful Iceland — and Grettir was a "greater fighter, and that such should be kings' men"(ch. 37). Grettir belongs, in other words, in a monarchy where great deeds are possible and sanctioned; in Iceland, he would undoubtedly have been taken to the Althing and outlawed or forced to pay compensation to Thorbjorn's kin. Again a subtext appears: since Iceland submitted to domination by Norway shortly before *Grettir's Saga* was composed, the author is raising a series of questions concerning the outcomes of this takeover. Will heroic Icelanders flourish again under a monarchy? Will peace be broken rather than restored — the Althing had deteriorated into a scene of battle as *Njal's Saga* describes. Or will violence without law replace the

Icelanders' legal effort to restrain their passions? Various answers suggest themselves as the saga evolves.

Grettir, unable to find a worthy opponent other than a ghost in Iceland, returns to a Norway governed by St. Olaf, who in addition to spreading the gospel, by reason if possible, by force if necessary, was rewarding and honoring men of prowess. But this voyage, like his first, is a disaster — Grettir has no place anywhere. The voyage is a terrible one, and the crew is freezing to death off the coast. They see a house with a roaring fire in the distance, and appeal to Grettir's pride to swim the treacherous, icy waters and fetch it for them, as no anchorage is nearby. Grettir reaches the dwelling, which in fact was "a house of refuge for men to rest in, who traveled along the coast" (ch. 38). But it is no refuge for Grettir. Covered in ice he seems to be an evil troll, and the inhabitants attack him before he can explain himself. During the fight, the house catches fire and twelve men are either slain by Grettir or burned to death. Grettir returns with some fire to his ship, but when his mates learn of the fight they disown him, fearing the punishment he will receive for the devastation: Icelanders have become ungrateful, unheroic, and far more concerned for their safety than loyalty to friends or justice.

Grettir does not hide, but goes before King Olaf and offers to undergo a trial by ordeal. He will hold a hot iron in his hand, and if it does not blister it will signify God's judgment that he is not guilty of intentional murder. But even the chance for justice is denied him. As he prepares to seize the iron, a "strange, wild lad" intervenes, shouting: "It is amazing that in this land, now that men are Christian, evil-doers and riotous people and thieves should go free through trials. Here is a criminal, who has burned innocent people, and yet he will have a trial to free him. What a custom!" Grettir responds in a fit of passion and strikes the lad dead in the presence of the court: perhaps the wild boy is another pagan ghost condemning Christian justice, or perhaps the saga is questioning the trial by ordeal as a system of law compared with the more rational deliberations of the Althing. In any case, King Olaf praises Grettir — "few men are your equal for strength and stoutness of heart" — but considers him "far too luckless to remain with us" (ch. 39). Grettir's great deeds are too much even for Norway — he appears like a troll or monster rather than a human being when he performs them. To confirm the irony, Grettir slays a berserk who is plaguing the farmer with whom he stays before he leaves the country (ch. 40). Despite their rejection of Grettir, the peaceful people need him.

Justice again fails Grettir when he returns to Iceland. His brother Atli, a prosperous and peaceful trader who has inherited the estate of their deceased father — a representative of the new Iceland as Grettir is of the old — has aroused the wrath of Thorbjorn Oxmain, another throwback to the old days, the only one who could control Grettir as a child. Thorbjorn was "a great and hardy warrior" but "notoriously cruel to his servants" (ch. 30). Envious of Atli, he planned to attack him; Atli's men foil the ambush, and Atli wins compensation at the Thing (ch. 43). But Atli's trust in a legal order based on real justice goes too far. He harbors one of Thorbjorn's mistreated servants, but then he is willing to turn the man out, as Thorbjorn has a legal right to his services. But then Atli is moved by a higher justice when the servant pleads: "I was sure you would not drive me away after I had worked so hard for you, and that you would stand up for me. This is breaking my heart. I will be beaten here before your very eyes if you do not help me" (ch. 45). Atli is no match for Thorbjorn, who kills him.

As Atli's closest blood-relative, Grettir must take the case to the Thing and demand either compensation or outlawry for Thorbjorn. However, Grettir was not allowed to do so, for Thorir of Garth, father of two of the men slain by the house-burning in Norway, used his great influence to have Grettir outlawed in his absence. Iceland's Althing ignored the advice of Law-Speaker Skapti: "A tale is half-told if one man tells it. This is an evil deed, and I do not approve of judging Grettir guilty" (ch. 46). "Many men" agreed the outlawry was "high-handed" and "illegal," but the action stood. If Norwegian monarchical justice was arbitrary, based on the king's whim and the ordeal, the much-praised Icelandic courts are no better. A poor servant can be mistreated, his protector murdered, and the rich and powerful run rampant over the voice of the law symbolized by the Speaker. Ironically, it is Thorbjorn Oxmain, like Grettir a man with little use for peaceful institutions, who now uses them against Grettir after murdering his brother who lived by and believed in them. Thorbjorn sets the unprecedently high price of three marks on Grettir's head as an outlaw. By having Grettir outlawed for a crime he did not really commit, and did not even commit in Iceland, by a man who had shown utter contempt for the law, the saga, like Grettir himself, is driven from pillar to post, from Iceland to Norway, in a futile effort to find justice.

Grettir then must wander Iceland with a price on his head, as he is equally an outlaw in Norway. He kills Thorbjorn (ch. 48), but even good men, like Grim (ch. 47) and Snorri the Priest (ch. 49) who offer him understanding and kind words, are afraid to shelter or openly defend him. He temporarily stays with a man named Thorgils, who is universally known for hospitality, even to outlaws, and lives in a remote location. But Thorgils is also harboring two brothers, Thorgeir and Thormond, who have an old grudge against Grettir's father: he had them outlawed for killing one of his kin in a dispute over a beached whale (chs. 24, 27). Nevertheless, Thorgils keeps the peace between the headstrong men: in fact, in this genuinely supportive environment, they turn their rivalry into games and contests of strength (ch. 49). Thorgils wins "great renown" for housing the "wildest men" and keeping them quiet (ch. 51). His safe-haven recalls the initial agreements among the great men who first brought order to Iceland without formal law. Where there is moral authority, mutual restraint, and an absence of scarcity and threats, laws are unnecessary. Where such conditions are lacking, laws do little good.

This point is poignantly made when Thorgils' peace is followed by the account of another Althing which refuses justice. Rejecting an appeal from Grettir's family, Skapti rules that Grettir could not prosecute his brother's murder as his outlawry preceded it, even though Skapti had previously admitted the outlawry itself was illegal! Snorri the Priest makes an effort to convince Thorir of Garth to release Grettir from the outlawry in exchange for remitting the fine Thorir must pay the rest of Atli's kin to satisfy Thorbjorn's crime. But Thorir replies, "Grettir will never get out of his outlawry": to encourage the murder of Grettir, Thorir doubles the price on his head to six marks. Snorri correctly predicts that "many a man would have to pay for the sport of keeping so potent a man an outlaw" (ch. 51). Deprived of the means of subsistence, Grettir once again turns anti-social, and begins "to sweep up unsparingly" the goods of small farmers (ch. 52). In their unyielding vendettas, the Icelandic chiefs not only made a mockery of the law but undermined the peace and security of average folk. When the great men were outlawed, the republic could no longer do the one thing it did well, protect the small from the ravages of the mighty.

To add yet another paradox, it is thirty such humble folk who succeed in capturing Grettir. But perhaps out of fear, or maybe the simple need to toil for subsistence on Iceland's rocky soil, none can spare the time to watch the "strong and crafty" man (ch. 52). No concept of self-sacrifice for the general good exists here, as Grettir spontaneously and generously exhibited on numerous occasions. They bring Grettir to the house of

Vermund the Slender, the local chief who is away at the Althing, for safekeeping until he can hang the outlaw. This event too is symbolic, for Vermund would have executed Grettir. But his wife, Thorbjorg the Big, tells her tenants: "Maybe Grettir is guilty, but it is too much for you to kill him, for he is a great man, with mighty kin." She sets him free on the condition he refrain from further violence in the area and promises not to avenge himself on his captors.

Thorbjorg's act is significant for many reasons. She is the first person in Iceland to give Grettir real help — and she is a woman. We are brought back to the saga's opening, where Grettir is reduced to womanly behavior. With only a woman standing up for justice and helping Grettir, Thorbjorg demonstrates the womanly status to which Iceland's men have fallen. Women make a belated appearance in *Grettir's Saga.* Thorbjorg is its first major female; the author has been saving her to make an important point. Justice is now to be found in informal communities and unusual places, outside the law if not actually out-lawed, rather than in the legal system.

Thorbjorg is the first person to place Grettir's immediate crimes in the context of his larger career and reputation. She doubts his guilt, and reasons beyond the mere fact of his outlawry to the truth that the Althing isn't working well, and that Grettir's relatives might come after her. But either way no justice is possible — she must either shortchange her own tenants to be fair to Grettir or punish a great man for petty crimes he was forced to commit. Thorbjorg's intelligent understanding of the multiple possible contexts of law and justice appears when she answers her husband, who rebukes her for freeing Grettir: "First, you will be considered a greater chief for having a wife who dared to harbor an outlaw; his kinswoman Hrefna would tell everyone that I would not let men slay him; and third, he is the man of the greatest prowess in many ways." Vermund thanks his "wise" wife for her advice (ch. 52). In her arguments, Thorbjorg realizes her husband's communal reputation is more important than an Althing that is turning into a playground for manipulation of technicalities and an excuse to run roughshod over justice. "Law" is not only what the court decrees, but a question of social legitimacy. The irrelevance of the Althing and Vermund's attendance there is reinforced by Thorbjorg's act of informal justice. Finally, the mention of Hrefna suggests Thorbjorg is at least as concerned with her reputation among Iceland's prominent women as she is with her husband's stature. This hints that women of the community do serve as moral enforcers who try to hold their husbands to a level of decency. In this chapter, too, the community of tenants — the poor — also appear as enforcers. The chiefs' Althing, it seems, left out women, the lower class, and great individuals like Grettir whom it increasingly outlawed and who began to form outlaw communities as well. The republic the Althing stood for was reduced to the corrupt tool of a quarrelsome aristocracy.

Grettir thus becomes more useful to the alternative communities, to the people on the periphery of Iceland's society, than he ever was when he tried to win the approval of the respectable and powerful. He uses his great strength and intelligence not to fight or engage in sports, but to build a bridge for his kinsman Thorstein Kuggson. But he complains a lot about the work, which Kuggson uses as an excuse to drive him away when Thorir of Garth learns of his whereabouts (ch. 53). Family rejects Grettir, as do "friends": he fends off ambushes from men who feign kindness, win his good graces, and then treacherously attempt to slay him. Thorir's silver is a powerful inducement to the many Icelanders who have no livelihood. Since Grettir cannot bear to be alone, he keeps trying to make friends despite his unfortunate experiences: his one true companion, Hallmund, is murdered by another outlaw as they quarrel over some fish (ch. 62). This whole part of the saga (chs. 53-63) offers a vivid picture of an outlaw's life: he cannot trust anyone, is shunted from one house to another by people who are kindly enough but unwilling to take risks or get into trouble — once they have used Grettir to help them out of *their* difficulties. Grettir takes up with other outlaws who are always a threat to turn in one of their fellows in return for the reward money and readmittance to society, and everyone knows Grettir has a high price on his head and Thorir of Garth would support his murderer.

The saga writer goes out of his way to show how devout Christians fail to extend to Grettir the charity he shows to them. Under the pseudonym of "Guest" he moves to the Sand-heaps. Tired of wandering, rejection, and looking over his shoulder, Grettir hopes to find a home if he remains incognito. But his true identity emerges when he helps a woman named Steinvor attend church on Christmas Day by carrying her and her daughter across a raging river, a feat only he could have accomplished (ch. 64). He then helps the local priest out by killing an evil troll which had been murdering people in the vicinity. The priest, however, who assisted Grettir by lowering him with a rope into the troll's cliffside cave, loses courage when he sees blood, assumes Grettir is dead, and lets him climb back up by himself (ch. 65). This betrayal foreshadows that of the general community, which expels Grettir the following spring when it learns Thorir of Garth is hot on his trail again (ch. 66). Steinvor gives birth to a child that summer, a strong lad like Grettir who did not resemble Steinvor's husband, but who died at age seventeen (ch. 67). Grettir can have no heirs in a settled society.

Grettir continues his reformation by refraining from killing the worthless son of Snorri the Priest. An enigmatic figure who is the main character of the *Eyrbyggja Saga* and also appears in the *Laxdaela Saga*, Snorri sometimes stands for justice, sometimes for self-seeking duplicity. Here Snorri has ordered the wastrel Thorodd out of his house with the warning not to return until he has performed a great deed. Thorodd's attempt to kill Grettir fails, but the outlaw spares his life; Snorri promises to help Grettir all he can (ch. 68), but Grettir's bad luck holds — Snorri dies before the next Althing (ch. 78). Snorri's death and the irrelevance of his good will is another sign that law and justice had become irrevocably separated. But Grettir's assumption of the mantle of morality is validated by the famous Snorri's acceptance. Like the English Robin Hood, whose legend was contemporaneous with the sagas, Grettir has become the doer of good and great deeds who wins a popular, posthumous victory over a perverted legal system.

Grettir's final abode is on the isle of Drangey. Once again, two rights are in conflict. First, the right of the island's legal owners to their property — and to be spared the wrath of Grettir's pursuers for their failure to do their civic duty by turning him in. Second, Grettir's right to live somewhere. The place belongs to a number of men who raise sheep there, but Grettir claims it and moves in with his younger brother Illugi, who idolizes him, and a worthless servant named Thorbjorn but commonly known as Noise (chs. 69-70). Here Grettir's real nemesis is yet another Thorbjorn, known as Angle, the most "riotous" and "wild" of men who killed his own step-mother when they were quarreling (ch. 70). As the three Thorbjorns — Oxmain, Noise, and Angle — show, the republic had not failed to tame malice and disorder, which makes Grettir's sufferings appear more and more arbitrary. Angle is an extreme version of the young Grettir, but he technically has the right to the property — a far cry from Eirik's hospitable reception of Onund Tree-Foot. When efforts to pay off Grettir to leave fail, Thorbjorn gets all the island's other owners to sell off their shares cheaply (chs. 71-72) on the condition he will kill the outlaw. This is easier said than done, for Drangey is set on high cliffs, which Grettir is able to dominate by constructing ladders which he pulls up at night or whenever he is threatened (ch. 69).

Before his final demise, Grettir achieves a brief, temporary peace. A saga convention is followed here: an alternative possibility in a healthy society is presented in contrast with a forthcoming disaster. Under his disguise as "Guest," Grettir attends the local Thing. Resuming the socially acceptable role of a sports competitor, he is a big success with his wrestling prowess. He then persuades the Thingmen, including Thorbjorn Angle and the other owners of Drangey, to grant him their peace, which they agree to as he is in disguise. They swear: "Let him be accursed who breaks the peace, turned away and driven from God, and good people of the Kingdom of Heaven, and all holy ones. Let him be cast out of churches, and from both Christian and heathen people, from houses and caves, and every home but the home of Hell" (ch. 73). But the oath means nothing to the Thingmen when they discover they have made peace with Grettir — the men think themselves generous in allowing him to go home to his island, for a faction led by Thorbjorn Angle would have killed him on the spot. The conflict between law and justice appears here in perhaps the starkest form in all the sagas. When Grettir appears not as "the famous outlaw" but as an anonymous "Guest," he is popular for both his personality and abilities. But the refusal of the Thingmen to accept common-sense justice and put their feelings and salvation over an outlawry verdict sixteen years old (ch. 69) signals the end of the sense of honor and decency which had to support legal technicalities.

It is Thorbjorn Angle's covenant with Hell, with the old pagan gods, which ends Grettir's life. He arranges for his foster-mother Thurid, a heathen and a witch, to carve runes in a piece of timber which she curses and sets adrift toward Drangey (chs. 80-81). Although Drangey is short of wood — Grettir has to make a secret trip to shore for firewood when Noise carelessly lets their fire die out (chs. 76-77) — Grettir twice spurns the driftwood as bewitched. But it comes back a third time, Noise finds it, and cuts it into firewood. Grettir, angry at his feeble strokes, seizes an axe without examining the log too closely: a piece splinters and wedges in his leg, producing an infection which saps his strength. Thorbjorn leads a party to the island. By chance, or because the spell is working, Noise has fallen asleep without pulling up the ladders.

Thorbjorn's men set on the servant, who prefers to save his life and remain silent rather than shouting a warning to Grettir. Grettir and Illugi put up a heroic defense against Thorbjorn's band of eighteen (chs. 83-84) but are finally vanquished. Thorbjorn offers to save Illugi's life if he swears to avenge himself on none of his brother's murderers — he knows an oath would mean more to the honorable Illugi than his own vow at the Thing. But Illugi is worthy of his great sibling: "I might consider it, if you had let Grettir defend himself fairly, and won with manliness and strength; but I would never, even to save my life, become base as you are" (ch. 85). By forcing Thorbjorn to kill him, Illugi augments his disgrace at so ignoble a victory and ensures Grettir's kin will have a better case for revenge than had the outlaw alone been killed. Thorbjorn even fails to collect the reward of six marks for Grettir's head: Thorir of Garth refuses to pay up on the grounds sorcery was involved. Thorbjorn in turn accuses Thorir of being a tightwad and stupid to boot (ch. 85). Such were Grettir's opponents: unable to keep their promises to each other, these respectable thieves without honor could only defeat the great outlaw after a series of incredible circumstances, brought on by witchcraft, enabled eighteen of them to overwhelm a man who was greatly enfeebled to begin with.

At the Althing, Thorbjorn is outlawed for as long as any of Grettir's and Illugi's kin survive, or probably for the rest of his life. Grettir's chief adversary has to take his place. Although Thorbjorn was technically within the law to kill an outlaw and his supporter, the Althing had finally decided to do justice, given Grettir's reputation and the shameful way he was trapped. Grettir's own life-work, fighting spirits and witches, is legalized: the Althing declares that "all workers of the old craft would be made outlaws" (ch. 87). This is the first time the Althing or the Law-Speaker does the right thing for the right reason. Previously, even Thorkel Moon had granted Onund Tree-Foot's sons the right to share Eirik's land on the grounds he must have paid for it (he didn't — ch. 12). Skapti took Grettir's father's side in a murder case because they were relatives, and redefined the law concerning ownership of beached whales to give landholders precedence over the original discoverer (ch. 27). Skapti had also advised the hiring of Glam and that Grettir move to Drangey. In a final criticism of the Law-Speaker's wisdom, Skapti's successor Stein ruled that Grettir had been an outlaw nineteen rather than twenty winters — outlaws were free after twenty years, although no one ever survived so long. Grettir was slain during the disputed year (ch. 79).

The disjunction between true justice, which an outlaw's heroism shames the Althing into finally accomplishing, and legal rules is driven home in the saga's epilogue. Afraid for his life, Thorbjorn Angle sails first to Norway and then to Constantinople, where he joins the Varangian Guard, as had many Norsemen. But he reckoned without the persistence of Grettir's brother Thorstein Dromund. Thorstein lived in Norway and had only made one brief appearance early in the saga, where he joked with Grettir that some day his thin arms would avenge Grettir's stout ones (ch. 41). With no ceremony, Thorstein locates Thorbjorn in Constantinople, at a weapons-show where he is showing off Grettir's sword and boasting of having slain him, and kills him (ch. 89). Unfortunately, he has no proof of why he was entitled to do this, and is sentenced to death for an act of true justice that every reader of the saga rejoices in.

Thorstein is freed, but again real justice is done by corrupting formal justice, and in a truly absurd sequence of events at that. A noble woman named Spes hears the condemned Thorstein singing in his cell (ch. 90). She pays off the judges and bribes his way out. They fall in love even though she is married, so she commits adultery. To escape her husband's charges of infidelity, she cleverly hides Thorstein and persuades her friends to lie that she is guiltless (ch. 91). Then she divorces her spouse, swearing before a bishop that she is innocent, and deserves a divorce because her husband has falsely accused her of doing what she in fact has been doing (ch. 92). We are reminded by these events that, as in Norway, justice in the Byzantine monarchy was utterly corrupt, and if Thorstein was justly freed it was only because he charmed a wealthy woman. Juxtaposed with what has occurred at the Althing, where after many years Grettir finally received justice and sorcery was outlawed, the saga could be telling us that under free institutions, justice at least has a chance if people are worthy of it.

Spes and Thorstein return to Norway, but King Harald will not take Thorstein for his man. Spes then repents of her deeds, and persuades her husband to go with her to Rome, where they live as penitents in separate cells for the rest of their days: "We have been very lucky in our lives, and maybe fools will try to imitate us because of our good fortune; let us make such an end that good men also may follow us and do the same" (ch. 95). The undeserved luck of Spes and Thorstein, who survive and prosper thanks to her machinations, constrasts vividly with the bad luck Grettir suffered all his days, especially after he began to do good deeds.

The saga concludes by bringing us back to Grettir. Sturla the Law-Speaker concludes that he was the "wisest" of men — surviving by his wits in outlawry longer than anyone else — the strongest and best for doing away with ghosts and evil spirits, and the only one ever to be avenged in Constantinople, which testifies to the devotion he inspired among his family (ch. 95). Grettir is posthumously vindicated, and formal and real justice are reconciled. Grettir left his mark on the law with the outlawry of witches, and also on Iceland's landscape: Grettir's Point (ch. 60), Grettir's Heave (ch. 76), and Grettir's Hillock (ch. 87) were three sites where he performed some of his greatest deeds.

But it is a bitter and unsatisfactory reconciliation. If we regard Grettir as the best of Iceland, a symbol of its republic and spirit — much like Gunnar in *Njal's Saga*, who was also outlawed for being too great for his contemporaries — then he encourages us to meditate on Iceland's strengths and its weaknesses. Iceland and Grettir are tragically destroyed by their greatness taken to extremes — a system of law that gets bogged down in technicalities, which encourages those who would do the right thing to ignore the law altogether. Can unjust law or just lawbreakers then be blamed for the breakdown in social cohesion and public morality? Should we condemn a corrupted society, fighting ever more bitterly over increasingly scarce resources — a consistent underlying theme of the saga — for distorting what once was a sound legal system and forcing the best people outside the law?

The Althing and its Law-Speakers are presented as unjust and unwise compared to the great outlaw. Is this the author's way of justifying the republic's self-destruction and submission to Norway in 1262? Or does the saga say — "look what you threw away" — Norway has no justice either: Saint Olaf denies Christian justice to Grettir, and his successor refuses to accept Thorstein Dromund as his man. We ultimately arrive in Rome with people who renounce the world and live as monks, but the most devout Christians in the saga — the Sand-heapers and Saint Olaf — are among the most unfair to Grettir. Grettir is undone through pagan sorcery and buried in the Christian church that refused to help him, symbolizing the fate of a republic which neither religion could save.

"Who showed you the way to the island," Grettir asked Thorbjorn Angle in their final exchange. "The Lord Christ," replied Thorbjorn. "No," said Grettir, "It was the cursed hag, your foster-mother." "It will be all the same to you, no matter whom I have faith in," was Thorbjorn's response (ch. 84). Thus it was for Grettir and for Iceland, a powerful and hopelessly intertwined mixture of Christian and pagan, vengeance and mercy, bravery and knavery, justice and malice. What remains are the stories of great and good men like Grettir, who tried to do justice and live honorably, though the combined weight of two religions, economic scarcity, a corrupt republic, and a tyrannical monarchy came crashing down upon them. The formal, pious concluding lines of the saga: ''Good people, here the work doth end; May all folk to the good God wend'' is not so much an affirmation of faith, but a searching invitation to think seriously about what is ''good'' and how can justice win out.

Chapter Four

EXCEPTIONAL WOMEN: *LAXDAELA SAGA*

Synopsis: Gudrun, the protagonist, instigates the murder of her third husband Bolli, whom she believes misled her into their marriage on the pretext that her true love, Kjartan, Bolli's former bosom companion, had abandoned her. The saga is the story of Gudrun and her four husbands, the opportunities and limitations for exceptional women in Iceland. An important second theme is that rumor and assumptions, rather than fact, propel the action: it is difficult to tell who is instigating events, only that they are happening. Gudrun is transformed from a naive young girl, to a vengeful harpy, to a matriarch, to Iceland's first anchoress and nun.

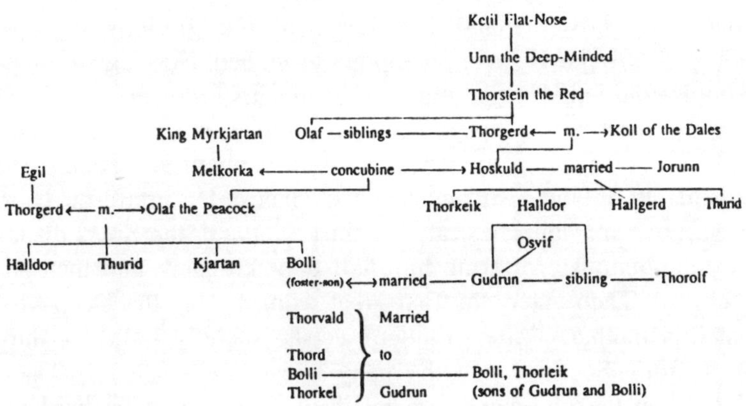

Laxdaela Saga considers the health and decline of the Icelandic republic from the perspective of women. Marriage, love, divorce, fidelity, concubinage, children favored and scorned, inheritance, and kinship are the primary issues which led to lawsuits and vengeance, which in this tale of the evolution of the Lax River region in the west of Iceland are derivative although important matters. Just as the male sagas test whether traditional legal and political arrangements were in fact

Icelanders' heroic efforts to balance freedom and order without coercion from church or state, the *Laxdaela Saga* examines the character of Icelandic women, who act the more usual dominant part of men while the men are distinctly dependent, weaker, and womanly according to traditional stereotypes. The saga thus questions those stereotypes.

Like the other great sagas, *Laxdaela* is open to several interpretations. It examines from multiple perspectives whether the extraordinary freedom women enjoyed in early medieval Iceland — able to manage estates, divorce husbands at will, hold chieftainships, and exert great influence if their intelligence and spirit were up to it — was one of Iceland's glories or a key factor in its downfall.[1] Alternatively, the republic's decline is reflected in the mirror of women's lives as great women turn from the founding and institutionalizing of the nation to quarreling over lovers and inheritances, ending up tamed in the bosom of the Catholic Church. The tragedy of Iceland becomes the tragedy of its women: strong females, like male heroes, are too big for the petty disputes and hard times of the later republic. Energy which in a better epoch would have gone into settling a region and uniting its leading families takes a destructive turn.

Like the other great sagas, *Laxdaela* opens with a prologue demonstrating how Iceland functioned in the glorious days of its founding. Ketil Flat-Nose is yet another prominent Norwegian forced out by King Harald Fair-Hair's tyranny. He tells his followers that they have only two alternatives, escape or death, as submission is not even thinkable (ch. 2). His sons go off to an Iceland — it is about 900 A.D. — where there is plenty of land, fish, and beached whales. His grandson Thorstein the Red, however, launches raids against Scotland; the Scots dispose of him by duplicitously offering him half their kingdom and then slaying him (ch. 4). Then enters the first great woman, Unn the Deep-Minded, Thorstein's mother. After his demise, she secretly builds a ship and escapes from Scotland "with many great noblemen." The saga comments on the uniqueness of her deed: "It would be hard to find another woman escaping such dangers with so much wealth and so many followers. This shows what a paragon among women she was" (ch. 4).

The woman's solution to the problem of how to deal with tyranny and Norway is thus shown to be superior to the man's. Thorstein leaves Norway only to start inflicting cruelty on others; the Scots treat him as he deserves. He represents an element in the Icelanders' souls — the desire to leave home and go off raiding like their viking forbears. But it is a defect to be corrected, not a strength to be praised. Unn must save her people, repeat her father's flight for freedom, and demonstrate that Icelanders cannot live as kings or in other kingdoms, but must create their own free society.

Unn sails for Iceland. She is greeted by her brother Helgi, who has preceded her. But perhaps he is afraid of her, perhaps provisions are already getting scarce — it is about 915. He only offers to house her and nine of her companions. She calls him "mean-spirited" and decamps to the estate of Bjorn, her other brother. He receives her well, but she decides dependence on men is not for her and leaves to settle the Hvammsfjord region in western Iceland near the Lax River. She distributes the territory to her kin and supporters for their "service and goodwill" (ch. 6), once again providing a positive contrast with a man, in this case her inhospitable brother. She makes substantial grants to loyal ex-slaves, embodying Iceland's purpose as a land of freedom and demonstrating the proper way to reward inferiors. Her last act is betrothing her grandson Olaf, who accepts the arranged match in the spirit which ought to have provided a model for Icelandic unions: "I shall only marry a woman who will not challenge your wealth or authority" (ch. 6). Many of the saga's quarrels occur when kinsmen's wives vie for pre-eminence, or unsatisfactory marriages are arranged. Unn holds an enormous feast to celebrate the wedding, endows Olaf with all her possessions, walks majestically down the hall to her bedchamber after ordering drinks for everyone, and then dies. The next day, Olaf confirms his status as a worthy heir by distributing "magnificent" parting gifts to his guests — the legacy of Unn to Iceland.

Olaf receives his estate at a time when Iceland was not yet fully settled and scarcity was still in the future. This ideal situation does not last long. When Olaf's brother-in-law Koll of the Dales dies, his widow Thorgerd leaves her son Hoskuld in Iceland and returns to Norway where she marries Herjolf: "she was an exceptionally capable woman, and Herjolf greatly added to his stature through such a wife" (ch. 7). Already republican Iceland, symbolized by its women, is adding to the prestige of its erstwhile mother country. But Norway is a potential snare for Icelanders: their frequent return trips and their intermarriages divide their estates and loyalties. Thorgerd begins this problem in the *Laxdaela Saga* by returning to Iceland, after Herjolf also dies, to stay with the boy Hoskuld. She loves him much more than Hrut, his step-brother, and endows him with Hrut's share of her Icelandic property, which the laws of both countries demand the boys share equally. The issue is temporarily moot, as Hrut inherited his father's large estate in Norway where his wealthy kin cared for him (ch. 7). But Thorgerd's marriages and decisions raise issues which, while not immediately threatening in Iceland's halcyon days, will return, with a vengeance.

Another difficult question is introduced, of marriage without true affection, but it too does not create disorder in Iceland's age of peace and prosperity. When Hoskuld grows up, he wishes to marry Jorunn, "an attractive, dominating woman of great intelligence, the best match in western Iceland" (ch. 9). Her father lets her decide for herself, a wise move which the sagas show tends to preserve familial and social order. Between this marriage and Olaf's, we learn that a well-made Icelandic union considers the wishes of the spouses as well as the parents, who are concerned more with wealth and reputation. Jorunn wastes no time demonstrating her "exceptional intelligence" by consenting to the marriage if it pleases her father — it does. She enters the union, however, more for the material benefits she can obtain from Hoskuld than for love. Paradoxically, by thinking like a patriarch rather than acting like a young girl in love, Jorunn also brings about a problem which will lie dormant for a while but eventually creates many difficulties. She and Hoskuld "usually got on well, but their relations were rather reserved" (ch. 9).

This time it is the trip of the man, Hoskuld, to Norway which complicates a situation which could have been contained had people just stayed in Iceland. He becomes a great chief, and travels to Norway for timber to build a larger hall. This journey, which many Icelanders undertake, symbolizes the growing scarcity of provisions in Iceland and the need to depend on Norway for recognition and survival. It also characterizes the desire of prominent Icelanders not to be satisfied with repute at home, but to seek favors and rewards from the kings of Norway, who are usually glad to bestow them in return for military help with rebellions and external wars. Hoskuld takes his time paying his respects to King Olaf, who is annoyed at this: "We would have accepted your greeting if it had come earlier, but we still do so now" (ch. 13). Nevertheless, Hoskuld gets away with his arrogance: the king rewards him with a sword, the timber he needs, and the bracelet from his own arm, commenting "you will be hard to replace." Hoskuld's trip is a paradigm for those of his son Olaf and grandson Kjartan: honor from the Norwegian king swells Icelanders' pride and encourages them to ride roughshod over the rights of their neighbors at home. Needless to say, such behavior does not impress the republican islanders, and leads to aristocratic pretensions which are resisted, chaos, the ultimate collapse of the republic, and finally submission to Norway.

While in Norway, Hoskuld also compensates for his loveless marriage by acquiring a concubine who appears to be mute. He brings her back to Iceland, where she bears his son Olaf, whom he names after the boy's great-uncle. Hoskuld discovers not only that she can speak, but that she is Melkorka, daughter of King Myrkjartan of Ireland (ch. 13). Women silent in Norway acquire a voice in republican Iceland. Jorunn is not happy, and Hoskuld sets up Melkorka and Olaf on a small farm he frequently visits after Jorunn beats her with a pair of stockings (ch. 13). Hoskuld's love for Melkorka parallels his trip to Norway. Iceland is intelligent, practical, hard-headed, its law concerned with the compromising of estates and neutralization of its people's turbulent emotions. Jorunn is all this, which is why Icelanders journey overseas for the adventure, romance, and glory of their viking ancestors. This is Melkorka.

Now the saga leaves Hoskuld's incipient problem with his half-brother Hrut and his marital difficulties to introduce yet another heroic woman, Vigdis, who is also a grandchild of Olaf, Unn's son. She honorably saves her distant relative Thorolf, "a penniless vagrant" who kills Hall, the "worthless" brother of the powerful priest Ingjald, as they quarrel over shares of fish they had caught together. Scarcity is setting in with a vengeance, and begets injustice. Hall attempted to cheat Thorolf by deciding unilaterally how the catch would be divided because he thought his high rank gave him that right; Hall's relatives pursue Thorolf even though Thorolf was legally defending himself from theft of his property. Already the high and mighty are pulling rank on ordinary Icelanders, even though they too must scrounge after fish and timber. But this early — it is about 950, and the Althing is now functioning — justice still gets the upper hand, although it is a woman of the middling sort who achieves it over a great clan.

Thorolf took refuge with Vigdis, not with her husband Thord Goddi, both because she was related to him and she was "a much more powerful individual than her husband." Vigdis's arguments for protecting him, over her husband's objections that Hall's clan will persecute them, reveal much about early, informal Icelandic law and justice: "I will not spurn our kinship, and you are not to be blamed for what you did," she tells Thorolf. Thorolf's honor required that he revenge himself on a man who cheated him. But the honor of Hall's clan compelled them to avenge Hall as well, even though they themselves admitted they were glad to be rid of him. Similarly, Vigdis's repute will be enhanced if she can successfully protect Thorolf, with whom she had little to do previously. Two sides are forming on a matter of honor and kinship, even though there are no emotional ties involved — another symbolic tale of how the Icelanders' tempers got them in trouble. Vigdis notes that "anyone harboring Thorolf is risking both life and estate, considering how important the opposition is." Nevertheless she takes the risk, commenting "my husband is no hero" and "we women always lack foresight." Still, she will do the right thing over her husband's objections.

Ingjald and his people show up to demand Thorolf, successfully bribing Thord with three marks of silver and waiving all charges of harboring a criminal to persuade him to surrender the fugitive (ch. 14). But Vigdis learns of their deal, has her strong and trustworthy slave Asgart spirit Thorolf across the Lax River, which Ingjald considers impassible, and frees Asgart for this heroic deed (ch. 16). While the men are corrupting justice, a slave has joined a woman in taking up its tattered banner. Ingjald wants his money back. Vigdis tells Thord to give it up, "since you earned it dishonorably." But in a surprise move, she brings out the purse, tells Ingjald to take it, and then punches him in the nose with it so hard that it draws blood; "she added a stream of mocking words, adding that he would never get his money, and to get out of their house" (ch. 15). The whole episode uses a woman to shame men who have forsaken their role as upholders of justice and the social order through cowardice, greed, favoritism, and arrogant aristocratic pretensions: a fair synopsis of why Iceland lost its republic.

Vigdis next divorces herself from Thord and claims half of his estate as compensation for his betrayal of a member of her family. Now the two strands of the story come together. Thord is related to Hoskuld and has received protection from him as a leading chieftain in the area (ch. 11). Thord offers to foster Hoskuld's illegitimate son Olaf, and make him heir to his substantial estate, if only Hoskuld can save Thord from Vigdis. Hoskuld agrees and pays off another Thord, Thord Gellir, who heads Vigdis's family and is also Hoskuld's own first cousin, not to back the divorce suit. Hoskuld speaks consolingly to Thord Gellir, and convinces him Vigdis had no "legal claim" nor "valid charges." Besides, "Thord could not be blamed for trying to rid himself of a disagreeable character his wife had suddenly thrust upon him" (ch. 16).

The dispute is thus ended, but reveals bewilderingly complex kinship ties and property claims that can only with great difficulty be sorted out even at this early stage in Iceland's history.

Two interpretations can be plausibly made of the Vigdis-Thord episode. The more appealing is that a just woman is undone through the collusion of powerful men — Thord bribes Hoskuld as he himself was bribed, and the local notables conspire to silence her. Vigdis now leaves the saga. But from the standpoint of an Icelandic republic which sought compromise and social harmony rather than the pursuit of vengeance to its logical and just conclusion, Vigdis is the trouble-maker, stepping outside her social role, and causing far-reaching complications that the men must settle. The second interpretation is not attractive to the modern reader, but given the increasingly misogynist attitude of post-republican Iceland and the ambiguities worked into all the major sagas, it must be entertained.

Hoskuld's lack of interest in justice rather than self-aggrandizement is confirmed in the saga's next episode. His brother Hrut returns from Norway to claim his half of their inheritance; he is a powerful lord favored by the king. Hoskuld refuses him, and presents the excuse that their mother should have consulted him, her legal guardian, before remarrying. Once again, Hoskuld would disparage a woman's privileges and independence. Hrut is impatient with technicalities; his men seize half of Hoskuld's cattle while he is at a feast, and they kill four servants who pursue them. Hoskuld prepares for a fight, but it is his wife Jorunn who persuades him to make peace, with a verbal barrage combining arguments from law, honor, and practical consequences. First, Hrut is legally right: "He would have been justified if he had seized the cattle sooner." In what must have been years of pent-up emotion over her husband's favoring Melkorka and her child, she adds: "He will not be deprived like some bastard over what is his birthright." Second, Hoskuld will gain little honor from killing a man of his brother's stature to revenge himself for people as "insignificant" as his servants. By his stubbornness, Hoskuld has placed himself in the impossible position in which he will either have to forego justice for his retainers or kill his own brother. Finally, Hrut has friends: Vigdis's clan was angry that Hoskuld and her husband had cheated her and were biding their time. Hoskuld is persuaded, Hrut is only too happy to make peace, and from then on "they lived in friendship" (ch. 19). The very name, Jor*unn*, signifies a worthy successor to the great Unn herself; by balancing and harmonizing three facets of Icelandic law — self-interest, reputation, and the legal code — which could easily be set against each other, Jorunn preserves the peace Unn instituted from Hoskuld's alien, aristocratic high-handness. A woman again assumes the manly role.

Hoskuld is not out of the woods yet. He must still deal with Melkorka. He has begun to neglect her, and she fears that her son Olaf will be disinherited. So she marries a "huge, powerful, immensely wealthy" man ironically know as Thorbjorn the Feeble (chs. 11, 20) on the condition he equip a ship to send Olaf overseas, for she thinks her father the King of Ireland will shower him with honor and wealth. Olaf, like many Icelanders, will seek overseas support for a reputation in Iceland, since he is illegitimate and he therefore cannot become a great landowner and chief on his own. His cause is just, as must have been those of his compatriots who went elsewhere to augment their wealth and standing in what was a poor and overcrowded island by the thirteenth century. But the reliance on foreign prestige and alien, aristocratic splendor dooms the republic, as the curses that fall on Olaf symbolize.

Things go well for Olaf as long as he remains abroad. He first goes to Norway, where if anything he is treated even better than Hoskuld (ch. 22). The king "bestowed so much honor on Olaf that no foreigner had ever enjoyed such esteem or treasures. Everyone remarked how handsome and distinguished he was" (ch. 20). The king unsuccessfully pleads with him to remain, as does the nymphomaniac Queen Gunnhild who had also seduced his uncle Hrut (ch. 19) — in an unfree society, all an exceptional woman can do is be an exceptional lover, the saga implies. Olaf sails to Ireland on the great ship they give him, and at age eighteen proves himself a better navigator and leader than the ship's captain. Faced with bad weather, the captain wants to determine the ship's course by majority vote. Olaf convinces the majority to give up that right and trust him, arguing that in a life-or-death situation the "wisest" are more capable than "fools" (ch. 21). This incident could be a hint that republican consensus works well in peaceful Iceland but not in overseas or crisis situations, or it could foretell that to survive, most men must recognize they are fools, and use democracy to follow their natural leaders.

Olaf is raised to even greater heights in Ireland. He fights so bravely for his grandfather that old Myrkjartan offers him his throne as "more able to rule than my own sons; we cannot find his equal in our kingdom" (ch. 21). But then Olaf intelligently turns him down to avert a civil war:

"better to have brief honor than eternal shame." Perhaps remembering the fate of his ancestor Thorstein the Red and the Scots, he again demonstrates his wisdom. Olaf returns to Iceland like a king in triumph: "He wore a coat of mail and had a golden helmet on his head. He carried a sword embossed with gold, a beautifully carved spear, and before him a red shield on which a lion was traced in gold" (ch. 21). Golden and red equipment received from monarchs will be a recurring sign in the saga of overweening pride which leads to disaster.

A poignant, unhappy note in Olaf's grand homecoming suggests all will not be well. In Ireland, Melkorka's old nurse recognized her jewels and regained her ailing health on learning her beloved child was alive and well. She pleaded to return to Iceland to see Melkorka, but Myrkjartan refused, which later greatly upsets Melkorka. This moving incident suggests that from a woman's perspective personal relationships are more important than the adventure and glory sought by Icelandic men. It also suggests that for all their influence and demonstrable ability at key points in the saga, women's wishes and the requirements of domestic life could not so much be spurned as thoughtlessly ignored. In their lack of concern for the old nurse, Olaf and Myrkjartan display the insensitivity that will destroy Iceland — selfish men pursuing heroics neglect their social obligations. Finally, more than any other episode in the saga, the old nurse's story suggests to me that the *Laxdaela Saga* was probably written by a woman. Would a man be so concerned with the plight of this faithful old servant? The story's content, read symbolically, tells us that women who have served their society faithfully ought not to be ignored or left behind, as men tell most of the surviving tales.

Olaf, known as "the Peacock" for the splendid attire he wears, is ready for marriage. It is now the bastard's turn to lord it over his father Hoskuld, and insist on a marriage worthy of someone who has just rejected the throne of Ireland. He reluctantly accepts Thorgerd, daughter of the great poet and warrior Egil, the hero of *Egil's Saga.* Egil is quite willing, but this embodiment of heroic old Iceland insists on his daughter's right to choose her own husband. Thorgerd also has the old Icelandic spirit: what matters to her is Olaf's illegitimacy in Iceland, not his international reputation: "You want to marry me to a concubine's son; it does not matter how extravagantly he is dressed" (ch. 24). But Olaf wins her over, not with his garments, but with his spirit and intelligence. He marches boldly into Egil's booth at the Althing, sits beside Thorgerd, and says, "You must think this concubine's son very bold for sitting next to you and speaking to you.'' She is his equal: ''I'm sure you have done far more daring things than speaking to women.'' They talk an entire day, and Thorgerd consents to the match. But it will be an Icelandic marriage among equals. It is Olaf's personal qualities, which come through despite rather than because of the flashy clothes and wealth he has obtained abroad, which win her over. She has put him in his place, strengthened the traditional respect for women over the foreign contempt recently manifested in the cruelty toward Melkorka's nurse, and preserved Icelandic, republican equality. Needless to say, Olaf and Thorgerd came to ''love each other very much,'' and ''everyone agreed that she was an exceptional woman.'' Only Jorunn refuses to join the general rejoicing, sneering: ''That bastard has enough money to make sure people remember him'' (ch. 24). Given the misfortunes ahead, this observation ought to have been noted, although it was not.

Until this juncture, Hoskuld and Olaf were able to contain quarrels that would later tear Iceland apart. They rejected thrones, accommodated illegitimate children, and did not let the impulses of offspring oppose their parents' wishes. Above all, they had the sense to listen to their women. . But when Hoskuld dies, things nearly fall apart. On his deathbed, he asks his legitimate sons — he also has a legitimate daughter, Hallgerd, the oft-married character in *Njal's Saga* — to share their inheritance with Olaf. Both are great merchants, and are willing to give Olaf the twelve marks the dying man requests. They assume this is in silver, but Hoskuld adds, after they have agreed, ''in gold.'' Olaf tries to placate his furious brothers by offering to share the cost of the funeral feast, but he undoes this generous gesture by making a speech at the Althing in which he invites everyone who wishes to attend. This prodigality with his brothers' fortune leads to the second greatest funeral feast in Icelandic history, at which 1,080 guests stay for a fortnight (ch. 27). Given the great wealth of all three brothers, and the fact that Olaf is not only showy but genuinely generous, he conciliates his siblings. He offers to foster his brother Thorleik's son Bolli, which in effect acknowledges his brothers' superior rank in Iceland, where ''he who fosters another's son is considered the lesser'' (ch. 27). He then wins Thorleik's esteem by ''loving Bolli like his own son.''

This new-found respect is crucial, for Thorleik's greed and pride become the primary new obstacle to peace. Olaf, who is full of honor from overseas, becomes the peacemaker, whereas his brother, a merchant who has no glory, is filled with anger. Thorleik shelters a family of sorcerers who sell him some fine horses (ch. 36), but then he insults a man named Eldgrim, who offers to buy them for an excellent price, by turning him down. Eldgrim tries to seize the animals when Thorleik is asleep, but Thorleik's uncle Hrut comes to the rescue. After offering Eldgrim other horses, which he turns down, Hrut stands and fights although he is eighty years old: "I won't allow my nephew to be robbed even though we do not get on" (ch. 37). He kills Eldgrim and "greatly enhances his prestige," but Thorleik is angry that he needed an old man to preserve his honor. The only people who stand up for justice regardless of the consequences in this saga so far are women, slaves, and old men, people who are marginal or negatively stereotyped. Thorleik takes revenge on Hrut by sending two of the sorcerers to curse him, which they do by chanting spells which kill his youngest son. Hrut takes counsel with Olaf, they kill the witches, but Olaf saves his brother by persuading Thorleik to outlaw himself voluntarily. Thorleik does not have much choice, for "Hrut was deeply upset and his sons were mighty warriors" who would come after him. But he and Olaf part "with the greatest affection" (ch. 38). The situation is temporarily saved, but Olaf's pride has infected his brother who is incapable of dealing with it. Leaving Iceland is the only choice for men who cannot keep their tempers in line. But issues of inheritance, sibling rivalry, honor, prestige, and scarce resources are becoming ever more menacing. Olaf and his brothers function after Hoskuld's death without the advice of women. Only when men reaffirm family ties, as with Olaf's fostering of Bolli and persuading Thorleik to leave, when Olaf buries his pride and plays the womanly part in putting domestic harmony first, is Iceland's tinderbox kept from exploding.

The story of Thorleik and the sorcerers at first glance is irrelevant, but it functions as do many such tales in the sagas. It gives the satisfactory solution to a dilemma through compromise and diplomacy, which later proves deadly when revenge is pursued. For just before Thorleik goes, Olaf makes the typically ill-fated trip to Norway, once again to build himself a more magnificent house (ch. 29). Here he meets a disagreeable but "rich and powerful" man, named Geirmund the Noisy, who compels Olaf to bring him to Iceland in return for his hospitality while in Norway. A morose and grumpy fellow, Geirmund nevertheless wins the affections of Olaf's daughter Thurid, and bribes her mother Thorgerd into persuading Olaf to go along with the marriage against his better judgment. The marriage fails; Geirmund, who has lost his wealth in

Iceland, tries to sneak out of the country and desert his wife and infant child, but when Thurid learns of this she rows out to the ship he is preparing to sail in, substitutes the child for Geirmund's treasured sword which she takes, and drills a hole in the ship's longboat so she cannot be pursued. Geirmund puts a powerful curse on Olaf's household: "May this sword kill the greatest man in your family, in the most hideous manner"(ch. 30). Geirmund, the baby, and his crew were all lost at sea. A second curse is also placed on Olaf. He slaughters his great four-horned ox in its eighteenth year when one of its horns broke off. A woman then appeared to him in a dream: "You had my son killed and returned him to me mutilated. For that I shall drench your own son in blood, the one you would least want to lose" (ch. 31).

Unlike the curse of Thorleik's sorcerers, the curses of Geirmund and the ox-mother's spirit are not neutralized. Whereas previously opponents had cared for each other's children in an effort to reconcile disagreements, neither Thurid nor Geirmund wish to keep the child of an unhappy marriage. Here, too, for the first time, women are behaving impulsively, corruptly, and selfishly — perhaps the saga's author realized that the contrast between good women and inferior men was becoming extreme. The curse for the murder of the ox is especially interesting, for its age of death is the same as Olaf's on his first trip to Norway. He returned to Iceland in splendor, to be sure, but mutilated by his great pride and foreign ways. At any rate, the curses represent the unresolved issues of inheritance, marriage, obedience, and honor in the saga of Unn's descendants. For all their faults, Olaf, Hrut, and Hoskuld have kept the peace; the great women they married and confronted have argued and acted for justice. We are admiring women for their manly behavior and vice-versa. Is the old Icelandic system of law based on compromise and payoffs to be valued? Or did it deny justice? By reversing the traditional roles of male and female, the saga forces us to think more profoundly about the virtues and weaknesses of the system — what if women carried on like men? Maybe they did in republican Iceland, and another reason for the submission to Norway was that men could not control their women or the feuds they started.

Amazingly, we have yet to meet *Laxdaela Saga's* protagonist. About two-thirds of the saga concerns the four marriages of Gudrun, "the loveliest and most intelligent" (ch. 32) woman in Iceland. Gudrun undergoes remarkable transformations from a girl manipulated without her consent, to a passionate lover, to a vengeful, wronged woman, to a powerful matriarch, to Iceland's first nun! Her life shows the limited choices and difficult circumstances facing a woman who might have been an Unn in happier times. Through her marriages, we see the disintegration of Iceland from a woman's perspective, for the marriages fail to work because the proper mixture of emotion, legality, prudence, and concern for parents and society are absent. The long prologue to what is essentially Gudrun's Saga — had she been a man it would surely bear this title — is thus necessary preparation so that we can understand the complex familial and women's issues which undermine the social order they had previously underwritten.

Gudrun's first marriage at age fifteen, to a wealthy older man who is obviously smitten with her beauty, is the worst case possible. Her father Osvif arranges the union because Thorvald offers an incredible financial deal in his ludicrous effort to regain his youth. Gudrun would take charge of all their money, be entitled to half the estate if the marriage failed, and Thorvald was to "buy precious things for her" out of his half of the fortune. Gudrun did not care at all about the money; she was furious at being married without her consent, so she tried to bankrupt her husband. She constantly berated him for not spending enough on her. When in exasperation he slapped her, she made a shirt for him that resembled a woman's garment; that he wore it was grounds for a divorce in Iceland. This occurred after two unhappy years, and she took her half of the estate plus the jewels. As Thorvald had in effect been acting like a woman, weakly submitting to his wife's requests — even slapping her was a feminine gesture — outfitting him like a woman was the perfect way to symbolize the end of a marriage he had undertaken without any thought to his reputation or a reasonable property settlement (ch. 34). Thorvald truly stands for the most degenerate vision possible of Iceland — a corrupt aristocracy where all men care about is satisfying their lusts for girls and frittering away their inheritances. Confronted with this situation, Gudrun cannot ask for justice, only to make the best deal for herself and escape when possible.

Gudrun's second marriage also lacks the care and consultation which accompanied those earlier in the saga. She impulsively convinces a man named Thord whom she likes to divorce his wife, "Breeches-Aud," because she illegally dresses like a man. They marry and are happy even though Aud sneaks up on her ex-husband one night and slashes him across the breasts for revenge. Thord appears to have been a rather submissive type, hence the success of his marriage with Gudrun. When

Gudrun's father Osvif offers to revenge him, which he will not do himself, Thord says Aud "only did what she had to do." The quick juxtaposition of the cross-dressers Thorvald and Aud suggests a society in turmoil where sex and marriage roles are confused. Thord dies prematurely doing an impulsive, stupid deed, perhaps to compensate for his past cowardice. He determines to single-handedly rid the neighborhood of witches who have been stealing and casting spells. After they flee, they put a curse on his ship which sinks in a storm (ch. 35). Thord's death, like Gudrun's marriages, symbolizes a society where action is taken without thought and weak men only bring on more trouble when they go out of their way to overcompensate. Curses only start appearing, and working, well into this saga. They can have no effect, or the sorcerers can easily be vanquished — as Thorleik's were by Hrut and Olaf — when society functions properly.

Gudrun's third husband is Bolli, Olaf the Peacock's foster-son. Here her fate, and her husband's, turns from the absurd to the tragic. She falls in love with Kjartan, Olaf's son, but the author is careful *not* to say that the feeling is mutual, but only that "it was generally said that Kjartan and Gudrun were an excellent match" (ch. 39). It seems from the context that he reciprocates her affections, but this is never stated. The saga at several key points will use this device of pointing out that information is common knowledge without saying it is true: the message is that the community is not wise or perceptive, or that it no longer is. People, especially women, ought not to rely on its consensus in guiding their lives.

At any rate, Kjartan prefers to journey overseas with his best friend Bolli in search of fame and fortune rather than to marry Gudrun at once. She tenders him the unprecedented, unwomanly offer to accompany him on his trip. He responds: "That's impossible. You have to take care of your brothers and your old father. So wait for me for three years" (ch. 40). For all his virtues and the legacy of his great women ancestors, Kjartan, one of the most outstanding men in all the sagas, cannot comprehend a non-traditional role for his prospective wife — if she is that.

In Norway, the affable, beloved Kjartan undergoes a change of personality. The typical curse of Norway on Icelandic would-be heroes takes a special toll on him. He responds to King Olaf's preaching of Christianity by proposing to Bolli that they burn him in his house! When the king's spies hear of this, Olaf confronts an arrogant young man who admits to the plot but still refuses to change his faith. Only after a powerful Christmas sermon by the king does he convert, and he still refuses Olaf's request that he spread the gospel back in Iceland (ch. 41). Kjartan is out of his depth; a much-honored and flattered youth in Iceland, he assumes he will continue to get his way and throws all honor away as soon as the king suggests he change his religion.

That Olaf too was capable of using force comes home after his first missionary to Iceland, Thangbrand, is abused by the Icelanders. So Olaf holds Kjartan and three others as hostages until new missionaries can persuade Iceland to see the light. Instead of begetting peace, Christianity is accompanied by force and intimidation, and will lead to Kjartan's and Gudrun's tragedy. Is the saga making a not-so-veiled comment about the effect of the new religion on Iceland? In any case, Bolli returns to Iceland without Kjartan, and the trip has affected him too. Smitten with Gudrun himself, he stresses that Kjartan "is at the court of Olaf enjoying more honor than anyone else" (ch. 42) and is rumored to be the lover of the king's sister Ingibjorg, who gives him a magnificent headdress for his intended spouse, "the most valuable treasure ever to enter Iceland" (chs. 43, 46). However, in keeping with the saga's new tone in which rumors and innuendos propel the action and motivate the characters, Gudrun's relationship with Kjartan is not definitively known. Nor is Bolli's motivation in giving Gudrun this information — does he genuinely believe Kjartan intends to remain in Norway or is he simply out to catch Gudrun while he can? Like the characters in the saga, the reader must navigate in a confusing situation where lies not only abound, but where we do not even know what the lies are.

Bolli's courtship of Gudrun is initially unsuccessful. "I will never marry anyone else as long as Kjartan lives," she affirms, and as a widow she has the right to marry as she pleases. But she listens to her brothers and father who stress Kjartan's dallying and Bolli's desirability. Succumbing to pressure from the community, from men, Gudrun's fate again illustrates how social morals have deteriorated. Early in the saga, fathers insisted their daughters consent to advantageous matches. Bolli, on the contrary, ignores his foster-father Olaf the Peacock's warning that a loveless marriage will fail: once more we are reminded that the successful marriages of the past were accompanied both by love and parental consent.

Kjartan does return to Iceland after the people accept Christianity. He is wearing the tell-tale garments that he is favored by royalty and thus has changed from a republican Icelander into an arrogant aristocrat: "He brought out the scarlet clothes King Olaf gave him and put them on in all their splendor. He girded on the king's sword, wore a gilded helmet, and at his side carried a red shield with the Holy Cross emblazoned in gold and a gold-inlaid spear" (ch. 44). That he arrives as a symbol of Christianity is most ironic, for he is "moody" and cold toward Bolli, whom he blames for stealing Gudrun: he refuses a gift of magnificent horses from him. Meanwhile, there was "little love" (ch. 43) between Bolli and Gudrun, and Gudrun is angry that Bolli seems to have lied to her about Kjartan's imminent return. Bolli responds, and we cannot know how sincerely, that he "told her what he believed to be true" (ch. 44).

Gudrun joins the foster-brothers in becoming moody and sullen. "Most people believed she still yearned for Kjartan," but whether she is grief-stricken or already plotting revenge is uncertain. As for Kjartan, he "showed no sign of emotion" when he learned of her marriage, and gives in without protesting to his sister Thurid's suggestion that he "do the right thing" and marry Hrefna instead. Is he secretly in love with Gudrun — had he ever loved her? — or is his pride injured that Bolli would have taken a woman to whom he thought himself entitled? Thurid says, "People say that you are still pining after Gudrun, their reason being that you no longer love your cousin Bolli" (ch. 45), but once again we have no explicit declaration of Kjartan's feelings. This is the only saga which refuses to state its leading figures' motives explicitly, and it only does so once Icelandic society and family relations have begun to fall apart. This situation makes Gudrun's jealousy and anger more understandable, as she cannot fathom the real intentions of either her husband or the man she loves. *Laxdaela Saga* also intimates that whereas the world is clear and straightforward to men, women who are puzzled by its incoherence and complexity reveal their superior intellect and intuition.

The quarrel escalates among Gudrun, Kjartan, and Bolli. Kjartan insults Gudrun at the annual feast their fathers hold by insisting that Hrefna replace her on the high seat. "She is always to have precedence as long as I live" (ch. 46), he proclaims, little realizing he will soon be killed and this will only occur once. Next, he denies to Hrefna the right to wear the beautiful headdress Ingibjorg gave to his intended wife: "I think it more important that Hrefna own this treasure than that the guests have the privilege of seeing her wear it," he arrogantly declares. In this saga, it is the women who are willing to let the headdress, symbol of Kjartan's affections, be passed from one to the other, while Kjartan refuses to signify the true nature of his love by having it worn publicly. Kjartan turns his back on family, friends, and community, insults them, and is brutal to Gudrun who still loves him — out of anger or jealousy (we do not know) because he just might love Gudrun.

Gudrun's brother does not let her treatment go unavenged. Thorolf Osvifsson steals Kjartan's treasured sword, the gift of King Olaf, and buries it in a bog, suggesting symbolically that Kjartan ought to bury what he acquired in Norway as far as his personality is concerned. Kjartan recovers it without the scabbard, but refrains from taking revenge at his father's request. Next, Hrefna's headdress disappears, and "many people believed that Thorolf had burned it at Gudrun's request" — although we never know. Kjartan confronts Bolli to confess his complicity in the thefts. He denies any role, but Gudrun is more forceful: "You are stirring up a fire, Kjartan, which ought to be put out. You may be [note the ambiguity] right to say that people here have seen to it that the headdress disappeared. If so, they have only taken what was rightfully theirs" (ch. 46). Although she probably did not know it, Gudrun was the specifically named recipient of Ingibjorg's treasure.

The efforts of Gudrun's family to rid Kjartan of his Norwegian acquisitions to retaliate for the arrogance he learned there only backfires. Kjartan marches with sixty men to the house of her father Osvif and keeps the entire clan locked up for three days without access to their outside privy (ch. 47). They "were furious and much more humiliated than if two or three of the men had been killed." Kjartan then undermines justice by forcing a man named Thorarin to sell him some land already promised to Bolli, who really needed it to graze his livestock (ch. 47).

That nearly all the events from the supposed love of Kjartan for Gudrun are motivated by rumor is symbolized by the critical role of a woman named Thorhalla the Gossip. She lives with Osvif's family. After a conversation with Kjartan, she hastens to tell everyone she meets: "Never has he looked more elegant. It's not surprising that such men consider themselves above everything." She then adds that he enjoyed boasting about the land deal with Thorarin. Thorhalla's remarks prompt Gudrun to say "No matter what insult he inflicts, no one dares to stand up to him" (ch. 47). Yet Thorhalla's role creates some sympathy for Kjartan, and provokes reflection on the extent to which he may be a victim too — returning to find his bride taken, he is envied by people who resent the wealth and honor he received in Norway.

Gudrun finally does stand up to Kjartan, and insists others also do so. "You have the temper of peasants' daughters — you never do anything about anything," she taunts her brothers. "You have the memory of hogs," she adds, over Kjartan's insults, and is amazed when they fail to attack him when he is traveling about with only two men: "You just sit around pretending to be men, and there are always too many of you at home" (ch. 47). By questioning not just her brothers' masculinity but even their membership in the human species, she is again taking the man's role of avenging insults. But she cannot provoke Bolli, who had always remained silent or defended Kjartan when he was verbally abused. He brings up his past friendship and their happy childhood at Olaf the Peacock's, but such vestiges of the vanished order are losing ground quickly. Gudrun threatens to divorce him if he refuses to strike at Kjartan.

Kjartan's arrogance in the face of danger does not diminish. He dismisses the twelve men with him — "that thief Thorolf will not mock me for fearing to travel without a crowd" — and ignores portents in dreams. He is sure Bolli will never repudiate their friendship and thinks little of the rest of Gudrun's relatives. They finally persuade Bolli to accompany them to an ambush: nine men attack Kjartan, who has only two companions, but he is winning the day despite a sword that keeps bending — a symbol that recalls the distortion of his personality in Norway where he received the sword, and reminds us just how merited his reputation must have been to begin with. The attackers finally convince Bolli, who has been hanging back, to help them: "He surely would not want to live with the infamy of having offered to help and then refusing to." When Bolli joins in, Kjartan, exhausted but only slightly wounded, throws down his sword: "It is a shameful deed, kinsman, that you are going to do; but I would rather be killed by your hands, cousin, than kill you with mine" (ch. 49). Twice calling attention to their familial ties, Kjartan's death is so noble that it causes us to rethink and question the way the evidence has been stacked against him the past several chapters of the saga. Bolli strikes the unarmed man dead: he dies with his head in Bolli's lap, and Bolli is instantly grief-stricken.

Gudrun is not. When she learns of the murder, she coldly remarks: "Tasks are sometimes mixed in the morning. I have spun yarn and you killed Kjartan." By ironically reassuming the role of humble woman, Gudrun is really establishing mastery over her husband. That women matter more is confirmed by her next comment: "My greatest happiness is that Hrefna will not go gladly to bed tonight." But in her vengeance, Gudrun has made herself both pathetic and tragic: this "exceptional" woman, afflicted through no fault of her own with three unsatisfactory husbands, can only find a perverse pleasure in denying to others the love lacking in her own life. Bolli speculates that Hrefna, who made no choice in her marriage to Kjartan and hitherto has been quite a passive character, will be equally unmoved. But he is wrong. As we are told in perhaps the most tender passage in the saga: "Hrefna was filled with grief but continued to bear herself graciously. She took no other husband and lived only a short time thereafter. People said she died of a broken heart" (ch. 50). Hrefna's true feelings and dignified mourning raise her to a greater esteem than Gudrun; in this confusing scenario a woman simply fulfilling traditional female expectations stands suddenly above the principal characters, who are hopelessly twisted by their plottings and imaginings. The final irony, that "people said" Hrefna died of grief, is presented in a context where it loses its irony. The statement "people said" has a ring of truth it has not had before.

Kjartan's brothers want to kill Bolli, but Olaf the Peacock, in his last peacekeeping act, stops them: "Bolli's death would not bring back my son." Having established himself as an Icelandic patriarch, Olaf is no longer the proud young man he saw duplicated in his returning son Kjartan. Instead, he persuades them to wreak revenge on the two sons of Thorhalla the Gossip who participated in the ambush, thus symbolically attacking the fact that rumors and gossip were responsible for the whole train of events. Olaf then tries to reconcile the families: Osvif's sons must remain outside the country for what will probably be the rest of their lives — as long as Kjartan's brothers and infant son remain alive — to prevent the logical parties from escalating the feud. Kjartan's brothers want Bolli exiled as well, but Olaf permits him to remain in Iceland — with his remorse — and insists that everything remain in order as long as he lives. But both his sons and his wife were "filled with hatred for Bolli, and felt that he had betrayed his foster-kin" (ch. 48). Olaf acquired "great prestige" for these court actions, but died three years later.

The first major court intervention in this saga and the compromise peace it represents is symbolized by a man near death. It plays a small and ineffectual role; unlike in most sagas, law stands at the periphery of the deep-seated feuds that motivate men and women. The courts, the implication is, matter little to women, if at all. The Althing's near-total absence from *Laxdaela Saga* may also be attributed to the close kinship ties of most of the major antagonists, who would have been prohibited by a sense of honor from airing the dirty family linen in public. *Laxdaela Saga* can thus argue either for the indispensability of Thing justice in maintaining peace, or its irrelevance in the many instances, involving women and close relatives.

After Olaf's death, the action deteriorates into a ferocious vendetta with Thorgerd, Kjartan's mother — showing her colors as Egil's daughter — leading one side, and Gudrun the other. Women have taken over completely, and the result is indiscriminate vengeance. Thorgerd's first victim is one Thorkel, an innocent bystander who saw the massacre against Kjartan being prepared but failed to warn him. Thorkel's is the logical reaction of ordinary folk to the feud between the prominent clans: "For all I care, they can do what they want to each other." He is primarily concerned with "getting a good view where we can enjoy the scene without the danger to ourselves." He represents the community which found Kjartan's prowess offensive: "Everyone praises him for being the most skilled in arms; he's going to need that skill now." He also thought that warning him would be useless, as curses and dreams had foretold Kjartan's death — if we remember earlier in the saga, curses only work if people permit them to. And after Kjartan's death, Thorkel mocked "the yellow and cowardly way that Kjartan threw down his sword and received his death-blow." Thorkel is the saga's representative of ordinary Icelandic opinion, a tale-mongering busybody only interested in great events for their curiosity and gossip value. His fate suggests that poor Icelanders ought to have taken an interest in saving their communities from the quarrels of the great families, for they too lost their republic. It is Thorkel's very insignificance that makes him a logical first target for vengeance. Thorgerd tells her men: "I cannot even imagine you would seek vengeance when the odds are not with you if you will not even repay a scoundrel like Thorkel" (ch. 52). Thorkel, like the Icelandic republic, the saga may be intimating, "met his own death like a coward"; Thorgerd was not satisfied, but "she thought this deed better than nothing."

Thorgerd next takes matters into her own hands. She rides with her sons to Bolli's farm, and reminds them of their kin and ancestors: "You are remarkably unworthy of your noble kinsmen if you do not want to avenge such a brother as Kjartan.'' She notes that her own father, the great Egil, would never have been so cowardly, wishes her ''craven'' offspring had never been born, and taunts them, as Gudrun had her kinsmen, with attacks on their masculinity: ''You are more suited to have been your father's [not her] daughters and been married off.'' These goadings lead her sons to break the peace made by their late father Olaf — the keeping of which was an alternative tradition, the one stressed earlier in this saga, which Thorgerd overlooks. We have also reached a pass where we do not know who to blame for what — great women are now the leaders of blood-feuds they had averted in the saga's prologue. Are these women doing justice cowardly men will not, or are they destroying society and descending to the level of men? Are the men cowardly for not taking vengeance, or for being goaded by maddened women to renounce sensible compromises which keep order?

Olaf's sons finally form a party to attack Bolli, but Thorgerd insists on coming along. Without her, she thinks they will back down. Gudrun is a worthy adversary. She is tending sheep with Bolli when the group descends; she wishes to remain, but he sends her away. After the murder, one of the band takes Gudrun's sash from around her waist ''and wipes the blood off the spear which had run Bolli through.'' Symbolically, is the blame hers? Gudrun reacted by smiling and chatting with the husband's murderers (ch. 55). What was she up to? She had not gotten on with Bolli, and was perhaps secretly glad he was dead. Was she trying to undercut their satisfaction by showing that she, too, the instigator behind the death of Kjartan whom they were avenging, shared their joy? Or was she just biding her time, as Halldor, one of the group, says: ''I think she came with us because she wanted to learn precisely who had taken part. Gudrun surpasses all other women in courage and resolution'' (ch. 55).

Gudrun now demonstrates yet other of her outstanding characteristics. She calls in her friend Snorri the Priest, and suggests they exchange homes. Since he is also involved in a feud in the region of Eyr where he lives — discussed at length in *Eyrbyggja Saga* — he agrees. Snorri seems to be the peacemaker who will end the feud, but his efforts are no more successful than Olaf the Peacock's. Gudrun keeps demanding revenge, and after twelve years Snorri agrees to support her. She wants to strike at Kjartan's brothers, but Snorri dissuades her; they are too important and ''their relatives would pursue vengeance to the utmost.''

Also, Snorri is hoping "to end these family feuds once and for all" by coming up with a compromise that will slake Gudrun's thirst for vengeance yet not offend Olaf the Peacock's sons. So they settle on the murder of Helgi Hardbeinsson, one of Bolli's killers, and as Gudrun has no remaining powerful kin, they plan to use the "meddlesome, vain, arrogant, and overbearing" Thorgils Holluson to do the deed. He is madly in love with Gudrun, so she and Snorri promise that she will wed no other man in Iceland, a nice subterfuge since they are planning on a match with Thorkel Eyjolfsson who is currently out of the country (ch. 57). Snorri is engaging in his characteristic elaborate maneuvering, and Gudrun proves her mettle by advising and proving his equal every step of the way. To bring about a settlement, they have to do yet more injustice.

Gudrun's primary concern is vengeance. She insists her young sons, Thorleik, aged sixteen, and Bolli, who was born after his father's death, aged twelve, participate in the murder. She goads them much as Thorgerd had her sons twelve years before. When they say they are too young, she taunts them that they care more about "sports and horse-fights" (ch. 60). Thorgils then bullies two of Bolli's killers into joining the plot against Helgi. Their rationalizations for such treachery go far toward explaining why Iceland was reduced to a scene of carnage. One of them, Thorstein the Black, says, "there are important people concerned in this, people of stature [Snorri, Gudrun, Bolli's sons] who have felt deprived of their rights for a long time. We can hardly expect they will forego vengeance." Vegeance is worth taking to save yourself from the wrath of prominent people, even if it means repudiating your kin and duty. Thorstein adds: "I'm quite sure most people would rather sacrifice anything than their own lives. This is paramount, and one must deal with it first." By saying "most people," Thorstein hides his act by taking refuge in a postulated consensus of cowards — is that what Iceland has been?

Lambi, the second man approached to join in the scapegoat murder of Helgi, offers the excuses that he is at least saving his nephews — Olaf the Peacock's sons — and besides Helgi is a berserk, a threat to order they were better off without anyway, even though he was quite useful in murdering Bolli (ch. 59). Olaf's sons do not accept these arguments when Lambi, after Helgi's murder, tells them they should be grateful that he saved them from being killed. The boys inform their uncle the blood of Thorbjorn the Feeble rather than King Myrkjartan runs in his veins, and

Lambi and his nephews depart furious with each other (ch. 65). Gudrun has only killed one of her husband's murderers, but she has shown her influence in fragmenting the heirs of the great clan descended from Unn and Bolli and exposing them in their present state as cowards who think like "most people." They prefer dishonor and not risking their lives to any semblance of loyalty to family or justice, however defined. As an aftermath of the murder of Helgi, Snorri disposes of Thorgils by giving the son of the man from whom Thorgils had stolen his chieftainship an axe and suggesting he use it on Thorgils (ch. 67). Double-crossing the man who executed their vengeance, Snorri and Gudrun have hit rock-bottom, symbolizing the deterioration of Iceland prior to the republic's end, where powerful families unconcerned with any semblance of honor wreaked havoc in ever wider circles.

But Snorri and Gudrun did have a plan. For in the last chapters of the saga a new peace begins to be forged. Gudrun marries Thorkel, and the author goes out of his or her way to emphasize it is her first marriage in which not only the parties agree, but families and community approve: "My sons, Thorleik and Bolli, have the greatest say, but I will also accept advice from you, Snorri, for you have always advised me honestly and well" (ch. 68). Snorri's reasons for suggesting the match are practical: Thorkel "is most likely to become the leading chieftain in the west of Iceland," and is respected in both Iceland and Norway. Having abandoned any hope of love after Kjartan, the hard-headed Gudrun now is swayed by such arguments. By foregoing romance and the impetuosity which gave Iceland both its heroism and its feuds, pragmatic order can be reestablished, although the heroic age will end.

Nevertheless, Gudrun is still the boss, contrary to the dream she had when we first met her in the saga (ch. 33) that her fourth husband would "completely dominate" her — dreams, like curses, only work if people submit to them. She wastes no time in taking charge. An outlaw shows up at the wedding feast, asking for protection. Thorkel would do the legal thing, and turn him in, but as Gudrun has a much larger following than her husband, she insists they protect him, even though Thorkel had promised a great friend, whose brother the outlaw has killed, to take revenge. Snorri can only shrug his shoulders: "You can see for yourself what an incredible woman Gudrun is, when she gets the better of both of us." Overriding Icelandic law which demands punishment of outlaws, the wishes of her husband, and the obligations of his friendship, Gudrun protects the outlaw for no other reason — she has no previous connection or obligation to the man — than to symbolize that henceforth she will run things, and not Snorri or Thorkel, who are the two most powerful men in the west of Iceland (chs. 69, 70).

Under Gudrun's and Snorri's aegis, however, the feud among Kjartan's and Bolli's clans end. The younger Bolli marries Snorri's daughter Thordis. Once again the young people are happy and their union is sanctioned by their parents. Gudrun's reason for agreeing to the match provides another illustration of her forceful personality: "It is not only because I love him above all others, but also because he has always been the most faithful of all my children in obeying me" (ch. 70). Men are judged by Gudrun as they give her the unquestioned authority husbands tried to assume over wives. After Bolli's wedding, he and his brother scheme to renew the feud with Olaf's sons — it has now been eighteen years since their father was murdered. But Icelandic law makes a successful, if belated appearance in this saga: Snorri finally achieves "a good and lasting settlement." Olaf's sons pay compensation for Bolli's death, and Gudrun's sons foreswear vengeance. They exchange swords and shields to cement the bargain.

But they did not live happily ever after. This would be too facile an ending to so titanic a saga. The desire for glory and wealth felt by the descendants of Unn and the Irish kings could not be given up. The younger Bolli wants to make his trip to Norway, too. Snorri tries to dissuade him — "there's a grave risk in how this might turn out for you" (ch. 72) — and points to previous turning points suffered in Norway by Bolli's ancestors. Snorri offers Bolli a chieftaincy and large estate in Iceland instead. But Bolli not only spurns Iceland — as did the great families and heroes of the sagas — he outdoes them all in his exploits, rewards, and arrogance. He becomes the first Icelander to serve in the Byzantine Emperor's Varangian Guard (ch. 73), which though not historically true is appropriate to the saga's development. Norway did not suffice for his glory, so he went on to Constantinople. Considered "exceptionally valiant in every hazard," he returned to Iceland even more magnificently than Kjartan: "His companions all wore scarlet and rode on gilded saddles. He wore clothes of gold embroidered with silk from the emperor, and over them a scarlet cloak" (ch. 77). He would only wear scarlet or gold-embroidered silk henceforth, and was known as Bolli the Proud. The saga makes the subtle point that wherever he went "the women paid no heed but to gaze at Bolli and his men in all their splendor." Iceland's women had changed from the days when Egil's daughter Thorgerd was not taken in by Olaf's outfit, and he had to woo her with gentleness and wit. From Bolli's demeanor and the women's reaction to his company, the future appears to hold more feuds, with which the saga does not deal. But Bolli's journey occurred around 1026, and Iceland still had a quarter of a millennium of troubled republican history ahead of it.

Thorkel, Gudrun's last husband, also indulges in a parallel hubris. He duplicates his ancestors' voyage to Norway for timber, although this time to build a church rather than his own hall. But pride is still the motive. King Olaf gives him an enormous sum of money, a beautiful cloak, and all the timber he wants. But Thorkel repays this kindness by measuring the magnificent church Olaf has just built and taking enough wood to construct a larger one. Like Bolli, this Icelander also represents the spirit that enough glory is never enough. We see Thorkel's fate, however, in the saga. He is warned by Olaf, "You are a very remarkable man, but you are getting above yourself, and it is sheer effrontery for a peasant's son to compete with us." No church, the king states, "could contain your arrogance." (Was Gudrun the hidden hand behind his desire to build such an edifice?) In any case, a storm drowns Thorkel with all his timber (ch. 74).

Just before Thorkel's death another sign emerges that feuding might start up again. Thorstein Kuggson, a cousin of Thorkel, wants to buy some land from Olaf the Peacock's son Halldor, who is now impoverished after paying his share of the compensation for Bolli. But Halldor will not sell, which enrages Thorstein who is ready to strike him. Thorkel urges restraint: "it would be an outrage" to fight during Lent, and, more pragmatically, Halldor's last faithful slave Beinir the Strong is standing by to help his master with an axe (ch. 71). Again, we are reminded justice and honor came not from the high and mighty, but from non-citizens of the republic like slaves and women. But Thorkel told his cousin to wait until after Lent had passed and a more opportune time for revenge arose. We are left with this issue unsettled, as Bolli the Proud also is unleashed on Iceland. Was the peace of Snorri no peace at all?

An alternative to another cycle of vengeance exists. Gudrun prolongs the Lent which Thorkel mentions, symbolically speaking, by becoming a nun. She grows "deeply religious," the first woman in Iceland to learn the Psalms, and becomes the first nun and anchoress as well (ch. 76). Yet she did not lose her character. When a ghost appeared to tell her of Thorkel's death with the ambiguous words, "Grave news, Gudrun," she retorted: ''Then keep quiet about it, wretch'' (ch. 74). People can shape their own destiny, we are reminded, and she can go on whether her husband, whom she ''came to love dearly'' (ch. 69), was alive or not. Refuge in the church and scholarship is another possible destiny for Iceland, the one, historically, it in fact enjoyed. After the republic came submission to Norway, piety, and the sagas. Gudrun's son by Thorkel pays a pilgrimage to Rome, undertaken with humility rather than to bring back timber or to add to his personal glory. Her grandson becomes a man of great learning, following in Gudrun's pioneering footsteps. If her elder sons were heroes, her later descendants were priests and intellectuals. By the saga's conclusion Gudrun, having undergone numerous personality transformations indicative of the nation's progress, may be considered a symbol of Iceland itself. If Iceland ceased to be heroic, its reflection on the meaning of the turmoil of the republican age through the sagas was necessary to preserve its heroism for future generations. Did Iceland, like Gudrun, reach its true greatness in its final stage? Or was Gudrun's final metamorphosis the sort of sardonic anticlericalism which would have provoked mirth: Iceland's first nun was a four-times-wed, vengeful, conniving woman. The saga does not say.

Shortly before she died in 1060 at nearly ninety years of age, Gudrun was asked by her son Bolli which of her four husbands she loved the most. She replied: ''Thorkel was the wealthiest and greatest chieftain; no one was more accomplished than Bolli; Thord was the wisest and greatest lawyer; of Thorvald I have nothing to say'' (ch. 78). Gudrun has mellowed; she speaks only well of men she dominated and frequently treated badly, and with her feeblest husband takes refuge in silent discretion. The woman, nun, and scholar has created the myth of Iceland's golden age for her son, since when reading the saga we learned of these men's weaknesses. Among three of the spouses we have a composite of Icelandic virtues: political power, martial prowess, and legal wisdom. But Gudrun is silent on the question — whom did she love? Is she telling us Iceland's women loved none of them, or is her praise reflective of a saga tradition which glorified men and left out the women? So Bolli asks her again, and now she answers: ''I was cruelest to the one I loved most.''

Gudrun raises several issues with this brief, ambiguous answer. First, for the only time in the saga, at the very end, she admits that she too may have been wrong. As the embodiment of Iceland, its religious faith, and its scholarly pursuits she has begun the process of questioning her past, a far cry from the days of the republic when people thoughtlessly took vengeance and had trouble accepting alternative viewpoints. Second, given the unfortunate fates of all her husbands — and of Kjartan, who may well have been ''the one she loved most'' even though he was not her spouse — she ends the saga on a note of uncertainty, inviting the auditor or reader to perform this inquiry for himself or herself. At the saga's conclusion, Gudrun invites us to read it over again, from the perspective of an aged sage pondering the significance of her life as well as from the angle of a woman, beginning at age fifteen, in the process of living it. We are thereby asked to mull over the feuds, the marriages, the characters, and the role of Iceland's remarkable women in its remarkable history, a tale that *Laxdaela Saga* has ensured will never be forgotten.

Chapter Five

THE POET: *EGIL'S SAGA*

Synopsis: An extremely difficult, strong, and poetically gifted child, Egil leaves Iceland for numerous adventures in Scandinavia and the British Isles. Overseas, his poetry and strength must serve the ends of arbitrary kings. When he settles down in Iceland in his forties, he becomes a peaceful patriarch, and his art more genuinely expresses emotions of love and friendship. *Egil's Saga* is contrasted with *Gunnlaug's Saga*, where a poet dies an early, violent death by using his art in the obsessive pursuit of romantic love.

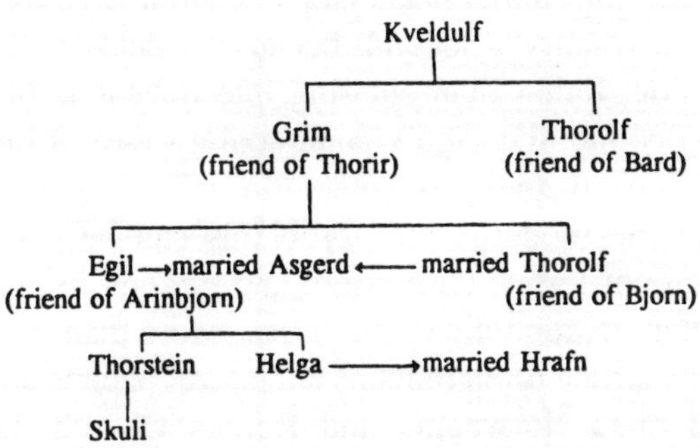

Egil's is the saga of a great poet who is also a tremendous warrior, a monumental drunkard, and a wealthy landowner. If he seems an unlikely poet, we need only think of the great poets and writers since the nineteenth century — Lord Byron rushing off to help the Greeks win their independence; Vallejo's, García Lorca's, and Hemingway's support of the Republicans in the Spanish Civil War; the extravagant lifestyles of Rimbaud, Baudelaire, and Poe; Rosa Luxemburg's and Emma Goldman's espousal of the Russian Revolution; George Sand and Isadora Duncan — whose lives merge with their work into their legends. The writer as political activist, the person who would test the limits of experience, is far more common than the bookish intellectual at work in his or her room.

Egil's Saga includes other poets — such as his great-uncle Olvir Hnufa and Audun the Fake-Poet — as a means of demonstrating the role of the poet, the writer, in both monarchical Norway and republican

Iceland. Egil is a symbol of Iceland. His father is one of the land's pioneers, and Egil contains within his person nearly all the contradictory characteristics of that great yet troubled nation. A courageous fighter, expert wordsmith, skilled legal tactician, and agricultural patriarch, he is also a murderous, conniving, greedy, stubborn, out-of-control, vengeful individual. Representing his country in all its diversity, Egil exemplifies the literature a republic of free people produces. The result is head and shoulders above the output of the Norwegian court poets compelled to praise tyrants.

Egil's Saga is unusual for two reasons. First, it is set exclusively in pagan Iceland. Egil dies at age eighty in 990, just before the island converts to Christianity. The saga thus also tests the viability and justice of Icelandic institutions under paganism, unencumbered by the complicating factor of Christianity. Second, because it deals with the period of Iceland's founding, rather than entering into questions of the republic's corruption and decline, the saga's main action reverses the usual pattern of its relationship to the prologue. In most sagas, a golden age demonstrates to the moderns how problems can be solved. In *Egil's Saga*, a prologue of terror, corruption, and tyranny in Norway prepares the way for Icelandic, republican solutions. More than in any other saga, Iceland's unreconstructed republicans and secret pagans could have taken pride in *Egil's* once Norwegian and Roman Church domination was firmly established by the end of the thirteenth century.

The saga begins with the story of Egil's Norwegian ancestors. These are people like himself who are immensely talented and will brook no interference with their personal freedom. Indeed, something is superhuman about them. Egil's grandfather Ulf was said to be a shapechanger and known as "Kveldulf" or "Evening Wolf." His great-grandmother was the sister of a man know as "Half-Troll." Kveldulf married the daughter of a friend who was a berserk: they went out raiding and "shared their purse." But then Kveldulf — who recites at least one poem — settles down, much like Egil will. He too has a split personality. He is a figure of "great authority," an extremely capable farmer and craftsman, and much respected for his counsel by all the people in the region. But as the day wore on he became more and more disagreeable and had to keep to himself. The two aspects of his behavior went to his sons: Thorolf was "generous and cheerful," beloved by all. Grim, Egil's father, known as Skallagrim because he went bald early in life, was a huge, ugly man but also a tireless worker: farmer, fisherman, craftsman, and blacksmith, blessed with tremendous strength; he too declaims poetry (ch. 1).

In Kveldulf's time, King Harald Fair-Hair was consolidating his rule over Norway. *Egil's Saga* depicts him as a despicable tyrant. He kills the other kings in Norway, even burning one of them in his house, a cowardly way of fighting, according to the sagas. Those men who did not accept his "tyranny" and "slavery" and did not flee the country met terrible deaths by having their arms and legs hacked off. Freedom-loving Norwegians soon colonized parts of Ireland, France, Scotland, Orkney, the Hebrides, and Iceland (chs. 3, 4).

The king is angry that Kveldulf neither visits him nor pays him allegiance. But his wrath is tempered by the presence of Kveldulf's son Thorolf and brother-in-law Olvir Hnufa. Olvir's misfortunes illustrate the plight of a poet who does not put his talents at the service of liberty and good men. First he falls in love with Solveig the Fair, composes innumerable love poems to her, and gives up the viking life of pillage and plunder to court her. But her family objects, tries to kill him, and forces him to escape to the only convenient refuge: King Harald's court. There he joins Audun the Fake-Poet as two of the king's three most trusted advisors, and has the unhappy task of trying to calm the king's wrath at his freedom-loving relatives, while also persuading them to accept royal supervision. A tyrant needs insincere poets to praise him, and Olvir's career illustrates the problem of artists and thinkers serving political ends. Incidentally, the saga does not quote any of his poems. First Olvir is the slave of a woman, then of a king (chs. 2, 4, 5). The difference between his poetry and Egil's will demonstrate the opportunities for talent a free society opens up.

Thorolf, Kveldulf's son, agrees to attend King Harald and become his henchman, for his courtiers enjoy "unequaled honor" in the form of "power, promotion, and privileges." Such words appear often in the young man's speech justifying his move, suggesting that Thorolf is genuinely attracted to the court, instead of responding to the king's threat that either Kveldulf or one of his sons must remain as royal retainers. Kveldulf and Grim, on the other hand, offer to "show the king friendship," but insist on "governing on his behalf in the manner they have for his predecessors." They insist on adhering to a traditional king-vassal relationship which Harald has made obsolete: he would own all the lands, have them governed by royal stewards who saw that taxes went directly into royal coffers, and keep all the powerful nobles at court to keep an eye on them. He was centuries ahead of Louis XIV (chs. 5, 6).

Kveldulf warns his son Thorolf not to be ''too ambitious.'' He should never try to equal men greater than himself — especially the king, it is implied — but never let them trample on him either (ch. 6). But while Thorolf is indeed a trustworthy and effective servant of the king, obtaining far more tribute from Finnmark and Lappland than his predecessor and fighting bravely in battle, he is destroyed through the slanders of the illegitimate sons of Hildirid. Their hatred of Thorolf arose because his best friend Bard had died in battle, leaving his entire fortune in Thorolf's hands to be given to his legitimate son Brynjolf. When the boys Brynjolf fathered by his concubine Hildirid approach Thorolf, he sends them away unpleasantly: ''I heard you make the same demand of Bard, who called you a couple of bastards, so I don't think you have much right to an inheritance'' (ch. 9). Thorolf is not the likeable man he was depicted as before he went to the king's court: he is an active agent of his tyranny, fighting to extend his empire into Finnmark, and denying a legitimate if not strictly legal claim.

Thorolf inadvertently angers Harald by having five hundred of his own men prepare a feast for his sovereign, who has only brought three hundred retainers. While he temporarily placates Harald by offering him a magnificent ship he has just built, the Hildiridarsons see their opportunity. Significantly noting that Thorolf ''treats other men's money as though it were his,'' they accuse him of gathering such a huge throng to kill the king, for they insist he is stealing from the tribute he collects (ch. 12, 15). Thorolf refuses to take them seriously, trusting to the king's reasonable evaluation of his past performance: ''The king would never believe such lies without a scrap of evidence.'' (ch. 14). When Olvir tells him to beware, he responds: ''I won't waste words on the king if he'd rather believe the slander of evil men than the honest truth that I tell him'' (ch. 16).

The saga's moral is that the word and justice of kings cannot be trusted. As the instrument of Harald's arbitrary power, Thorolf is blind to the fact that it can strike anywhere. Flatterers like the Hildiridarsons can easily become the instruments of policy for a king, for Harald gathers favorites at court rather than letting free men govern themselves and advise him fearlessly. Yet paradoxically, they can also be viewed as the champions of freedom, forced while remaining in context of the Norwegian monarchy to have to fight treachery with treachery, visiting

Thorolf's betrayal upon him. But they too are courtiers, and the real moral is the impossibility of any justice in the intrigue of a court that is oppressive to begin with.

Believing that Thorolf is robbing him, Harald orders his two chief military leaders, Sigtrygg and Hallvard, to seize one of Thorolf's ships laden with profitable goods obtained on a voyage to England (ch. 18). Ignoring his father's advice, Thorolf now tries to compete with the king, and raids his possessions. The king attacks Thorolf. Despite the pleas of Olvir Hnufa and Thorolf's wife the king burns him and his men in their house: "I've no intention of fighting outdoors and losing my own men. There would be a great slaughter, and he'll be tough enough to defeat even inside, although he has fewer men" (ch. 22). Harald's treacherous attack is a back-handed compliment to Thorolf's courage and ability, even as it further characterizes the brutality and unconcern with honorable methods of conquest which established Harald's own rule. The poor poet Olvir's fate is if anything even worse. Begging the king to let him leave the court, as he had "no desire to sit with the men who murdered Thorolf" his kinsman, the king refuses as he will not relinquish such a great poet. Olvir, the would-be peacemaker who sold out to the king, is condemned to a life of praising his family's murderers.

But Thorolf does not go unavenged. His great friend Ketil Trout slays the Hildiridarsons, takes off for Iceland, and distributes land to his followers. Iceland is founded by men who give land to their loyal retainers so they too may be free, the reverse of contemporary Norway where the king is dispossessing freeholders (ch. 23). Thorvald, Kveldulf, and Grim also swing into action. Olvir suggests they ask the king for compensation for Thorolf's death, which is risky. But he would speak for them and win the king over. Grim goes in place of his father, with a band of twelve ferocious characters who embody the Norway Harald is trying to tame. The king offers Grim the opportunity to serve him as had Thorolf, but only hinting at the possibility that if Grim proved outstanding and "watched his step better" than his brother Thorolf he might receive some regal reward. Grim replies to this with an equal insult: if Thorolf were not a satisfactory retainer, his brother, who claimed to be inferior in every way, certainly would not be one. Olvir then hustles Grim and his men out of the hall before the king's wrath explodes: Harald quickly orders his men to set after them and kill them (ch. 25).

But Grim and his father have the last laugh. They slay the king's young cousins and military leaders before leaving for Iceland. The fight and voyage sap old Kveldulf's strength, but in a moving passage, his coffin, which is lowered overboard on the trip, washes ashore. He is buried in Iceland, where men like him who loved freedom could find a home (chs. 26, 27).

Grim now settles down, much as his father had done. He need not be a warrior in a peaceful, plentiful land. He is a great blacksmith, shipwright, and farmer just as his father was. The poem he declaims on reaching his new home says much about the difference between Iceland and Norway. Whereas after killing Harald's men he sang "The brave man's vengeance on the king is now completed. Wolves and eagles march through his kin, hacking them to bits and heaving them into the waves," in Iceland he praised the virtue of industry: "The smith must rise early to forge the ore, with air from the bellows aiding him. The hammer attacks the hot iron I forge while working the bellows" (chs. 27, 30). The only thing being "attacked" is everyday work.

Icelanders then demonstrate how they can resolve a problem which had earlier led to poet Olvir Hnufa's servitude to the King of Norway: a love affair. Bjorn is the "outstanding" and "talented" son of a Norwegian chieftain, who falls in love with Thora, the sister of another chieftain, Thorir, who is a friend of both Grim and the King of Norway. Bjorn flees for Iceland, deceiving his father that he is sailing to Dublin on a trading voyage. He is welcomed by Grim, who only later finds out that he is an outlaw — Thorir saw to that — who had eloped against the consent of her brother. Grim is furious, but Bjorn has become great friends with Grim's eldest son Thorolf, who resembles his uncle in his sunny and generous personality. Grim reluctantly agrees to accept Bjorn as a householder, and Bjorn returns with Thorolf to Norway where Thorir, too, with the aid of magnificent gifts, is reconciled (chs. 34, 35).

A second peacemaking occurs because Thorir's foster-son is none other than Eirik, son of the aging King Harald. At Bjorn's suggestion, Thorolf gives Eirik a magnificent Icelandic ship, built by Grim. The three young men become friends, and Thorir and Eirik attempt to soften the old monarch's heart toward Grim's family. Harald is obdurate: "They're all arrogant, they have no sense of respect, and have caused a great deal of trouble." He suspects the same of Thorolf, but heeding Eirik's pleas he grudgingly grants him permission to remain in the kingdom. Eirik soon succeeds to the throne, Thorolf helps him win great victories in Russia, and before Thorolf returns to Iceland the king gives him a huge axe, beautifully inlaid with gold and silver (chs. 36-38).

But travel abroad will be disastrous for Thorolf as it was for his namesake. An omen of this occurs when Grim tries to use the axe to sacrifice two oxen and it shatters. He then warns his son that "while your travels have given you a great reputation, stay here, take as much property as you need and be a great man. Much traveling leads to bad experience" (ch. 38). But Thorolf insists. Grim tells him to take the axe back, pointing out in a poem that "This fearsome weapon's edge has many flaws. It's a big warrior, but blunt and weak. I'll send the sooty shaft of this coward back. I don't need royal gifts." Grim in rejecting an unsatisfactory axe symbolically confirms Iceland's staunch independence of Norway. The implication is the island was better off when it did not rely on Norway to solve its problems, and that nothing Norwegian is much good.

Thorolf remains in the favor of King Eirik, but his father Grim's intuition is right. Thorolf undertakes repeated viking expeditions in the Baltic and on the European continent (chs. 46, 50), before dying in a battle he fights with King Athelstan of England to protect his throne from the Scots (ch. 54). We are told Thorolf is slain because he rushed so quickly into battle that few men could keep up with him, and thus he was surrounded and overwhelmed by the enemy. Ironically, Thorolf meets his death almost immediately after he and his brother Egil, who accompanied him on the expedition, received preliminary baptism in the Christian faith at Athelstan's request (ch. 50). The saga is undoubtedly hinting that foreign influence, especially Norway, and glory-seeking trips abroad did nothing for Icelanders, and they would have been better off tending to their farms. Egil never followed up on his baptism; unlike his brother who trusted in and fought for kings, he survived.

We meet Egil at the age of three. In a tale undoubtedly exaggerated for effect, his father Grim refuses to take him to a feast at his grandfather's house — his maternal grandfather Ingvald has joined Grim and many other refugees. "You don't know how to behave yourself when people are drinking," Grim tells the lad. "And you're tough enough to deal with when you're sober" (ch. 31). So the precocious boy navigates the woods and fields to grandfather's by himself, suddenly makes an appearance, and spins off two spontaneous poems. The first poem hints that his grandfather was "generous" in "granting gold to heroic men," and that he would find "no more brilliant three-year-old bard than" Egil. The second poem gives us a foretaste that the child who had already shown himself to be resourceful, disobedient, inebriated, and a genius was also greedy. It praises the old man for the shells and ducks' eggs Egil received as reward for his feats (ch. 31).

But if Egil can be astounding, humorous, and brilliant, he is also a threat to the social order the Icelanders have established. They do not go to war, as they did in Norway; they sublimate their aggressions in sports. But sports are too confining for an Egil. At the age of six, he kills a boy of ten or eleven with an axe out of anger when the older lad beats him in a ballgame. But such violence ran in his blood. A few years later, Egil and a friend are competing with Grim. They are wearing Grim down, and in a rage he picks up the other lad, smashes him to the ground, and kills him. Grim is about to do the same to his son when the boy's old nurse intervenes; still, she and Egil must run for their lives, and Grim heaves a rock in their direction which kills her. Egil then begins to dislike his father — is Iceland's peace only skin-deep, or does it take an exceptional misfit like Egil to disrupt it? Egil next begs his brother Thorolf to take him on his second voyage to Norway (ch. 40). When he refuses, Egil cuts his ship adrift, lets it float out to sea, and tells him worse will happen if his wishes are refused. Thorolf finally agrees (ch. 40).

If the incorrigible Egil is too much for Iceland, he cannot last in the subservient Norwegian state. Left behind due to illness as his brother took off for his wedding feast to Thorir's niece Asgerd, Egil recovers and takes a journey with some men of Thorir's household. They are temporarily stranded on an estate of the king, and offered only sour whey and curds to drink, for the steward is saving the ale for a reception the king will attend that night. When the king hears travellers are housed on the estate, he insists they attend the party. Angered that he and his companions were not only denied ale but told there was none, Egil gets drunker and drunker, more and more insulting, so the king's steward and the queen try to poison him. But he senses the plot, kills the steward, cuts his way out of the hall, undertakes a daring midnight swim to escape his pursuers, many of whom he kills, and ultimately finds his way back to Thorir's house. He is proud of his exploits: "I made a mockery of their Majesties' majesty. I've sent three trusty royal servants down to eternal Hell" (ch. 45). Eirik accepts compensation from Thorir for his men, but wants Egil out of his kingdom.

What a good king could have obtained from Egil appears in England, where Athelstan owes Egil and Thorolf the successful defense of his kingdom against overwhelming odds (chs. 50-54). Eirik, too, is a much more civilized king than his father, for from his perspective Egil's outburst at the feast is uncalled for. Eirik's behavior suggests why Icelanders would begin to return to Norway to reestablish trading, kinship, and property connections following Harald's death, and also why people like Egil and Grim, the truly great Icelanders, would be no more comfortable under a decent than a tyrannical monarch. The future will show that Eirik cannot remain uncorrupted by power.

Athelstan offers Egil anything he wants in his kingdom, but Egil wants what is rightfully his: "a good deal of money" from his brother's estate in Norway (ch. 55). Egil returns, confident that the king will ensure his "lawful rights" even though he is an outlaw there and Queen Gunnhild is his greatest enemy (ch. 56). Yet Egil is not as concerned about the rights of others: King Athelstan has left two large chests of silver as compensation to Grim for Thorolf's death, yet Egil refuses to give them to his father, although he repeatedly asks for them, on the grounds the old man has plenty of money of his own. That occurs after Grim, following Egil's final refusal, takes his own money and buries it in a bog. He prefers losing the money rather than that Egil, who represents greed, heroism, and stubbornness in about equal proportions — a fair version of the early Icelandic temperament — inherit it (ch. 58). Egil wants his rights, but even when it comes to his father, he is not at this time in his life concerned much about the rights of others.

Although Egil strengthens his case for the inheritance by marrying Asgerd, his brother's widow, and can count on the staunch support of Arinbjorn, his bosom friend and her cousin, he still must win his rights in court in Norway. Bjorn has died, and the king has given Asgerd's share of the estate to Berg-Onund, the husband of her half-sister. A "hard, unjust, and greedy" man, he bears a striking resemblance to Egil. They come to the Gula Assembly, where sacred ropes are stretched to establish the precinct in which justice is to be done and force cannot be used (ch. 56).

Nevertheless, Norwegian justice is in sad shape at this early stage, much like it is in Iceland in the sagas which take place later or in the period when *Egil's Saga* was written. Arinbjorn has the case rigged: two-thirds of the thirty-six judges are in Egil's corner. But everyone is aware a judgment means little if the king will not enforce it. Queen Gunnhild herself, who has been Egil's prime enemy since he killed her favorites and sons, supports Berg-Onund's arguments that Thora, Asgerd's mother, was a concubine, taken from her father's house and illegally married. Thus, Thora's daughter Asgerd is entitled to nothing. Arinbjorn argues that Bjorn had been reinstated following his outlawry by King Harald, and that the two heads of family — Thorir and Grim — were reconciled. Egil adds a poem, accusing Berg-Onund of thinking only of his "avarice," defends his wife's legitimacy, and urges the "true-born king" to accept his case. Gunnhild loses patience, takes the case out of the king's hands, and has her henchmen cut the ropes and chase Egil away. Fortunately no one has any weapons, but Egil pronounces a curse on anyone who settles on his property: they will answer to him for breaking "the laws of the land, the peace, and incurring the wrath of the gods." He is pursued by the king's men, who kill ten of his followers, but Egil rejoices that he has slain Ketil, the king's much-loved helmsman who physically resembles his master, for revenge.

As the king is out looking for him, Egil daringly kills Berg-Onund by pretending to sail out to sea, which causes Berg-Onund to leave his house undefended. Egil then pronounces judgment on Eirik and the Norwegian monarchy in general: "May the gods rid us of this royal thief. May he be hung for highway robbery," calling on Odin, Frey, and Thor to strike at a king who will not let men possess their property, and who desecrates assemblies (chs. 56, 57). In his rage, Egil sets up "a pole of insult" and carves runes into it, commanding all the "guardian spirits of the land" to know no rest until they have driven Eirik and Gunnhild from their throne.

Despite Egil's greed — he even writes a poem frankly admitting that "money, his fields, and his inheritance" are really behind his quest for justice (ch. 56) — he has become the scourge of royalty and the champion of legal institutions almost in spite of himself. The similarity between Egil and Berg-Onund suggests that in a corrupt monarchy, the avaricious man must rely on the favoritism of the court to have his rights, but an Icelander, a republican, trusts to law and the courts and is driven into a rage when they are disregarded. A sly subtext is provided by the fact Arinbjorn had fixed the court his way; perhaps we are dealing with competing systems of injustice where one's choice of method depends on whether one's friends are royal or aristocratic. That Arinbjorn's adversary yet rival in injustice is the evil Gunnhild — a nymphomaniac and snare to corrupted Icelanders seeking prestige in Norway in other sagas — and that King Harald has already burned men in their houses, makes it clear that Norwegian "justice" is arbitrary injustice. Iceland only reaches this stage in its decline after several hundred years of legal evolution.

Egil's curse works. Eirik must kill his seven brothers for the throne. Having denied justice generally, the wishes of Harald Fair-Hair and his favorite son are of no weight with others. But Eirik escapes and takes many of his retainers, including Arinbjorn, to England, where Athelstan finds it useful to settle them in Northumbria in return for their services against the ever-restive Scots. Intending to visit his old friend Athelstan, Egil is shipwrecked near Eirik's seat of York. Once again, Gunnhild and Arinbjorn plead opposite sides of a case — the queen that Egil be immediately killed, Arinbjorn that he be given safe passage. Arinbjorn's plea that he gave up all his estates in Norway to follow his king, that no credit can be gained from killing an enemy who has offered his head and thrown himself on one's mercy, that the king "twisted" the law to rob Egil much as his father had driven Egil's family out of Norway "for no more reason than the slander of villains," and finally that Arinbjorn himself will defend Egil if it means his own life, induce Eirik to yield. Gunnhild, despite her reputation as a sorceress, fumes in impotent rage. To further enhance the appeal of releasing Egil, Arinbjorn promises that Egil will compose an elaborate drapa, a twenty-stanza poem honoring the king, in effect submitting to him, if Eirik spares his life (chs. 59-60).

The poem Egil offers is one only a tyrant could love: Eirik is a far cry from the young man who was Thorolf's friend. Egil lauds a ruler "Who blazed a trail of blood until Odin looked upon the corpses," "Whose breath unleased torrents of battle," "Who earned his fame as his troops cut men down." In addition to defeating his enemies, Eirik generously shared the plunder with his retainers. Ironically, he is a king driven from his kingdom for his abuses and living at the sufferance of a just fellow monarch. Whether Eirik realizes this or not, however, the saga does not say. Egil escapes to Athelstan, where he recites a poem he can believe in: "That manipulator of justice, that lord of jackals will boast of his gift of Egil's head. But I kept it in spite, not because of him; I owe it to my courageous kinsman" (chs. 60-61). Egil, too, has to be a false subservient poet at court to survive. Of his three long poems in the saga, Eirik's is the only one which is not heart-felt. Its praise of blood and gore certainly fulfilled Arinbjorn's prediction that Egil's poem would make Eirik immortal (ch. 60). It honors him as their inscriptions honor the Assyrians' bloodthirsty rulers.

Again, Athelstan offers Egil command of the English army and large revenues, but the Icelander is single-minded in pursuit of his Norwegian estates (ch. 62). He hears that Hakon is a good king, and Athelstan's foster-brother to boot. But there is no justice in Norway. Hakon remembers Eirik's and Gunnhild's troubles with Egil, and only reluctantly permits Egil to take his case to court. Hakon does so not for the sake of justice, which Egil pleads for most eloquently, besides offering Hakon his support in a future war against Eirik which looms, but out of friendship to Athelstan. Egil takes his case to the assembly, but the current occupier of his estate, a retainer of the king named Atli the Short, whose brother Egil has killed in escaping from the previous assembly, calls twelve witnesses to swear that Egil has no claim to any revenues. Egil then, according to both "law and custom," challenges Atli to single-handed combat. Denied his rights through royal abuse on the first round, he is about to be undone by legal technicalities, and so poses an older, traditional law of trial by combat. He slays Atli, although once again he doesn't exactly fight fair: his sword strikes well but bites poorly, and he wins by biting Atli in the neck (ch. 65).

Still, the king refuses to give Egil the revenues from his land, and when Arinbjorn pleads for him, the royal wrath turns for the first time on Egil's friend, who had repeatedly courted similar displeasure to help Egil under Harald and Eirik. Hakon responds to his insistence that "Egil has the law on his side" by telling him: "I don't want him in the country, and you yourself can only stay here as long as you don't favor foreigners above me and my words." Remarking that Arinbjorn is devoted to his foster-son, the son of the exiled King Eirik, Hakon foolishly drives Arinbjorn into rebellion on behalf of Eirik's heirs by his threatening remarks. Even Hakon confirms the truth of Arinbjorn's warning to Egil: that "king's halls have wide entrances and narrow exits," and kings are all "bullies." So Arinbjorn himself reimburses Egil instead. Egil earned this by killing a berserk who threatened to murder Arinbjorn's nephew Fridgeir and marry his niece. Egil, in turn, had granted Fridgeir the berserk's substantial estate (chs. 64, 68). Friendship compensated for the absence of justice.

While in Norway, Egil undertook one final adventure which probably gave him his fill of monarchy once and for all, for upon its conclusion he finally stayed put in Iceland. King Hakon had been shortchanged on his tribute from Vermaland, on the Swedish border. He decides to send Thorstein, Arinbjorn's nephew, to collect it, even though — or perhaps because — Earl Arnvid has been murdering his envoys. Egil is staying with Thorstein at the time, and decides to repay his friend. "A man of Thorstein's rank is not obliged to run such petty errands," he tells the king's men. Much like his grandfather Kveldulf's response to Harald, he states that Thorstein is willing to accompany the king as needed on his expeditions, and to supply whatever men he asks for. The king's men agree to leave Thorstein behind if Egil will accompany them instead. He agrees, and on the way avoids various treacherous plots on their part and Earl Arnvid's to murder him. In the most amusing, or disgusting, of these, depending on your taste, he becomes incredibly drunk at the house of one Armod who refused to serve him food or liquor. After the man's wife and daughter prove more hospitable, Egil vomits all over his stingy host, and finally gouges out his eye. He slays the king's treacherous envoys, informs him that Arnvid had been doing likewise and withholding money, and thereby reconciles Thorstein to his monarch (chs. 70-75). But having to serve an unjust monarch and his equally unscrupulous retainers to help a friend was not Egil's kind of task. He returns to Iceland, the wanderlust out of his blood and his greed finally satiated. In Iceland "he left others in peace and, a very wealthy man, ran his farm exceptionally well" (chs. 66, 76).

Egil is about fifty years old when he settles permanently in Iceland. Here, he writes his greatest poems: one expressing his grief that two of his sons have died, the other a hymn of praise to Arinbjorn. The combination of Arinbjorn's unselfish payment of money the King of Norway owed to Egil and the young men's deaths have purged Egil of avarice. Egil's poem about his sons opens with several stanzas about how difficult it is to compose verses under such a strain. Egil was contemplating suicide and his art saves him. But it is art of a totally new sort. One of his sons drowned: "Could my sword take revenge on the sea, I would fight the gods themselves," he proclaims: Egil has realized his courage and martial bravery are useless. So is his gold: "The tempest has stolen my greatest treasure," he laments. Good sons, a family, are more important now than his estates in Norway. All that is left to him is old age, and death looms, but Egil resolves to face it "with a stout heart." Similarly, Egil's poem about Arinbjorn praises his friend's generosity and heroism in saving his life: "Great Arinbjorn's wealth flows to his fellows like a flood." Egil contrasts this with kings whom he makes "the object of his scorn." An Icelandic patriarch, wise in the ways of the world, Egil symbolizes the viking who settles down and becomes, at least for a while, a peaceful farmer (ch. 78).

Egil also passes on his art to a young poet named Einar, whom he meets at the Althing — which Egil now regularly attends. Einar wins the King of Norway's favor with his verse, and receives from him a magnificent shield he gives to Egil (ch. 78). But the shield is eventually damaged, tossed accidentally in a whey-tub at a party. So is a magnificent silk gown Arinbjorn gave to Egil, which Egil's son wears to the Althing in the old man's stead although he is much too short for it. The stable Icelandic republic Egil and his contemporaries have established, worthy of honor from kings and nobles in Norway, will soon be lost through carelessness, trampled upon at the Althing like Arinbjorn's gown (ch. 79). Slaves are escaping and rebelling when Egil returns to his farm (ch. 77); they are Irish, a sad suggestion Icelanders have not learned to bestow upon others the liberty they themselves fought for against King Harald Fair-Hair. Egil's son Thorstein becomes involved with a "rough, ruthless, hot-tempered" (ch. 80) man named Steinar who insists on grazing his cattle on Thorstein's land. When Thorstein kills two of Steinar's slaves who pasture them there at his orders, Steinar gathers support at the Althing in the hopes of outlawing Thorstein for killing the men (chs. 80, 81). Injustice has moved from Norway to Iceland, overbearing men use their clout to obtain biased verdicts, and the struggle over scarce land and resources on an increasingly poor, overpopulated island has begun.

But the tragic end is delayed. Instead of breaking up into a brawl like the Norwegian assembly, Egil and Steinar's father — who bears the name Onund as did one of Egil's principal Norwegian adversaries — take charge of the case. An Onund in Norway, like an Egil, would find legal procedures and negotiations useless in achieving peace or obtaining rights. In Iceland, the family heads identify with the law. "We ought not to be present while our sons squabble at the Thing," states Onund. "It's a scandal, and we will look like fools if we cannot make peace between them" (ch. 81).

Egil's last Thing appearance is a blaze of glory. He rides to the assembly sporting a golden helmet, shield, and spear at the head of eighty men in case Steinar planned to force the issue. Symbolically, Egil who once battled for kings can now fight even more magnificently for justice in the Icelandic republic. The elevation of a poet and his poetry to a higher plane in a free society is paralleled by the symbolic use of Egil's appearance in armor: a republic transforms the real wars of monarchs to the struggle of free men for justice and a better life.

But the saga leaves open whether Egil is really striving for justice or simply using force to intimidate his opponent for selfish ends. Egil's old friend Onund agrees to let him be sole arbiter of the case, but Egil insists on strict justice. He rules that Steinar "disgraced his family," which had originally received the land from Egil's father, by consciously commanding his slaves to let the cattle graze on Thorstein's hay. Egil rules that not only did Thorstein have every right to kill the slaves, but that peace would best be kept by forbidding Steinar access to his farm in the area, rather than enforcing the law that stipulated outlawry for killing another man's slaves (ch. 82). Onund calls the verdict "utterly unjust" and promises trouble ahead for Thorstein, but Steinar's efforts to ambush Egil's son fall through. Steinar finally moves out of the neighborhood (chs. 83, 84). People can get their rights in Iceland, although it will be difficult and eternal vigilance is required. Egil's verdict is harsh by Icelandic standards — given Onund's eagerness to compromise, a settlement more satisfactory to both parties would have been the norm. But Egil is right that peace could not be kept with Steinar in the vicinity; his justice may be partial, but it is also pragmatic.

As an old man going blind and deaf, and, as he laments in a poem (ch. 85), losing his virility, Egil is bullied by the kitchen servants and appears headed for a pathetic death. He evens wishes to serve a king to escape the hearth, an ironic reversal of his earlier life which foreshadows future Icelanders seeking glory in Norway. But he surprises everyone. He tells his niece and her husband that he intends to take King Athelstan's silver — the compensation for his brother, the rightful possession of his father — and distribute it to the assembled crowd at the Law Rock. Egil has turned from a miser into a benefactor of the community, although he cynically remarks: "I will be surprised if they divide it fairly. I predict they will start pushing and shoving, and maybe even fighting." Egil is describing the ultimate degradation of Iceland in symbolic form. The just republic, represented by its Law Rock, will turn into a scene of violence as men quarrel over limited resources. The greed Egil has renounced for justice and communal benefit will take over as it had in Norway, and in his earlier life.

Egil's niece thinks his bequest "wonderful," but her husband terms it "insane." So old Egil borrows two of his nephew's slaves, has them hide the money, and then kills them, all of which he admits. But the money was never found. Egil's heirs are torn between loyalty to family and devotion to community; the Althing will come apart because people put their familial responsibilities ahead of their respect for law. But that Egil himself had so partially determined the case between his son and Steinar suggests that it could not have been otherwise. Iceland's decline could be delayed but not avoided: like the classical republics of Greece and Rome and much as the Founding Fathers of the United States would later predict for America, Iceland could only endure when civic virtue successfully checked corruption and avarice.

After Egil's death, his bones were removed to a churchyard when Christianity came to Iceland. Not surprisingly, a priest's effort to crack his huge, rock-hard skull with an axe was utterly futile (ch. 86). Christianity was not equal to the great Icelandic hero. Nor was monarchy. The saga concludes with a list of Egil's outstanding descendants — some handsome, most ugly, all great fighters and many poets among them. The final one to be mentioned is his grandson Skuli, who fought against King Olaf Tryggvason, the Norwegian King who brought Christianity to Norway and then to Iceland. Skuli took part in the battle which killed Olaf (ch. 87). Olaf, remember, imposed Christianity by force. An Egil, or his surrogate, a peaceful farmer and man of letters in a free society, a law-abiding patriarch, will always show up to get his rights against arbitrary power. At least, let us hope so.

Egil's Saga ends on a hopeful note that he and his noble descendants could still be an inspiration to Iceland around 1230, when it was written, probably by the great Snorri Sturluson. But the *Saga of Gunnlaug*, known variously as Worm-, Adder-, or Snake-Tongue, the poet who courted Egil's granddaughter and Thorstein's daughter Helga, is the story of what really happened to Iceland. Gunnlaug and Hrafn are two poets hopelessly smitten with Helga. She loves Gunnlaug and her father permits her to marry him, despite misgivings concerning his tremendous arrogance and hot temper, provided he goes abroad for three years and comes home a more civilized person. Whereas in Egil's day the Icelandic republic settled the spirits of poets and outraged victims of injustice, his successors cannot find peace and ease at home and must journey to the continental monarchies. Detained for two more years through no fault of his own, Gunnlaug is angered when Helga and Hrafn are married on his return. He then demands Hrafn duel him for her; they cannot in Iceland, which holds one of the greatest Althing assemblies in its history to outlaw dueling for the express purpose of keeping these young men in line. They sail to Norway to fight their battle, and the king also outlaws duels.

By this time, Gunnlaug and Hrafn have become objects of jest in several countries. People play games pretending to be Gunnlaug and Hrafn and egg them on to fight. They finally do so in Sweden. In a horrible and treacherous duel, Gunnlaug chops off Hrafn's leg. Then as the dying man begs for a drink of water, he strikes Gunnlaug down; he too dies three days later. Thus, two heroic and poetic Icelanders are alternatively ludicrous and lethal. If they are taken to represent their country, they teach us that the spirit of poets is the spirit of heroes and vikings, noble and admirable while fighting for freedom against Norway, but then left without outlets in peaceful Iceland. Egil managed to settle down, but his heirs could only follow the example of his headstrong youth. Gunnlaug's and Hrafn's feud then spills over into their families, who start a fight at the Althing and will take revenge repeatedly on each other. Although Helga marries a valiant, wealthy man who is also a good poet, she soon dies of a broken heart — for Gunnlaug. Here the saga ends, with destruction, chaos, and pining for the past.

Proud of their unique republican and poetic virtues, the Icelanders of the saga age recognized the fragility of their island's glory. Egil's renunciation of selfishness was challenged even in his lifetime, and Iceland could not contain the passions of its warriors, driven to compete for land, women, money, and sheer pride. *Gunnlaug's Saga* implicitly justifies Norwegian rule, for Iceland was destroying its best men. Like the heroes of the *Iliad*, like the young Egil demanding his rights in Norway, men who sought justice for themselves alone were condemned to be governed by force and passion.

Chapter Six

COMMON FOLK AND CHIEFTAINS: *BANDAMANNA SAGA* AND "ALE-HOOD"

Synopsis: Unjust confederacies of chieftains at the Althing conspire to deprive commoners of their wealth. The victims play off rivalries among the chiefs and appeal to justice and pity to win their cases.

Bandamanna Saga — usually translated as *The Confederates* — and the short story of Ale-Hood both center around an action at the Althing. A member of the common folk wins a case against a powerful confederacy of greedy chieftains anxious to rob him of his property. Written after Iceland had lost its independence in the aftermath of corruption and feuding among a half-dozen leading chieftains, who had reduced the courts and the inhabitants to dependence, these stories may be read in three ways. They may represent wishful thinking about the way the courts could do justice if only some of the powerful aristocrats subordinated greed to duty. Second, they show how divisions among the corrupted leaders provided an opening for clever commoners to obtain a fair hearing, although they too had to manipulate legal technicalities in unscrupulous ways to do so. Finally, the tales lament an Iceland symbolized by a properly functioning Althing, where talented if not always pleasant people could advance, survive, and have justice done them. An element of class resentment appears in the stories, too, for both Odd — the hero of *Bandamanna Saga* — and Ale-Hood are well-to-do merchants who have worked their way up and are not always well-liked by chieftains who have land, political power, and prestige but are short of initiative and money. Although *Bandamanna Saga* is slightly more complicated than the short, straightforward "Ale-Hood," both are highlighted by debates in which the verdicts in favor of Odd and Ale-Hood are denounced and defended. These verbal exchanges, institutionalized at the Things, provide an opportunity for the authors to indict the chieftains whose severing of justice and morality from law led to Iceland's decline.

Bandamanna Saga begins with a sketch of Odd's parents Ofeig and Thorgerd, who embody the early spirit of the island. Ofeig has land, but no wealth. He is cold to his son — stingy, as was Iceland with arable land and resources — but "a wise man and excellent advisor." With his wife Thorgerd, another "exceptional woman" as were so many in the sagas, he represents the virtues of the republic in its early days (ch. 1). Similarly, Odd stands for later generations who had to turn to trade to compensate for the scarcity they faced: he starts as a fisherman, then begins a freight-service, undertakes mercantile voyages abroad, and finally settles down and purchases a chieftainship (ch. 2).

Ofeig and Odd between them offer a compressed history of the island. There are troubles, represented by Ospak, "a big, strong, contentious man" (ch. 2), nephew of the outlaw Grettir, but he is controlled by Odd, who hires him. His strength is put to good use, he also prospers, and appears loyal to Odd. Problems begin when Odd undertakes a long trading voyage and leaves his chieftainship to Ospak when neither his father nor kinsman Vali, who is Ospak's foster-brother, wants the responsibility (ch. 3). Lack of dedication to the republic by its worthy men and trips overseas which increase the pride and wealth of those who make them are first steps in Iceland's fall. So are quarrels over women. Ospak is a good chief, but falls in love with Svala, whose guardian, Thorarin the Wise (ch. 4) lets them marry but refuses his approval. Unions which lack either love or the consent of prudent parents, as in other sagas, bode ill.

The dispute which institutes the saga's action occurs when Odd returns and insists Ospak hand back the chieftaincy. Ospak's honor, like Odd's, has grown. He claims to be ready to surrender it since he never wanted it anyway, but he insists that "normally chieftainships are transferred at public assemblies" (ch. 4). The next such assembly finds Odd absent, so Ospak attends and does the usual business. Now Odd is angry. On Ospak's return, Odd takes an axe, holds it menacingly, and threatens Ospak, who replies: "It's yours whenever you want it. There's no need to use force" (ch. 4). The facts are presented ambiguously, so it is impossible to blame either Odd for being overly aggressive or Ospak for reluctance to relinquish his power.

The two men never speak to each other again. After Ospak leaves Odd's residence, forty of his sheep are missing. Vali, the peacemaker and a good friend of both men — he may represent the introduction of Christianity to Iceland and its futility in solving its problems — tells Odd to forget them: "You won't be considered a great man if you let that trouble you." Ospak is angry that everyone blames him for the theft, and even Vali suggests — although we never really know — that he was responsible: "Don't lose your temper; I can see you've acquired much more than you could have by honest means." Odd rides to Ospak's farm with twenty men, Ospak prepares to meet them, but accidentally slays Vali, who resembles his kinsman. Even in death, Vali tries to achieve peace, and counsels Ospak with his final breath "to save yourself, you miserable wretch." He can do this by sending his wife to Odd, admitting his guilt, and having her tell Odd that Vali is travelling on business (ch. 4).

Carrying Christian forgiveness to Vali's lengths might have saved Iceland, but it is impossible as a general rule. Odd demands compensation for his kinsman Vali from Ospak's father-in-law Thorarin at the next Althing. Thorarin is reluctant to take the part of a man he and his friends agree was "a total scoundrel," who committed murder and then left his father-in-law to suffer legal action. But Thorarin is won over, less by arguments that this is his familial and legal duty, and more by taunts that he will be considered a coward if he refuses. Perhaps most important, as his fellow-chieftain Styrmir notes: "It would be a good idea to let Odd know that he is not the only important man around here. He keeps trampling on us and our followers and he always gets all the credit" (ch. 5). Odd, a *nouveau riche*, is a threat to the old, landed power structure; his eagerness to get his chieftaincy back from Ospak suggests their contention of arrogance has some truth.

Odd's case against Ospak, as even Thorarin realized, was airtight: Vali was totally innocent and Ospak had no reason to kill him. But he loses his case on the smallest technical point imaginable: he chose a tenth juryman at home, and only after one of the original group had died, rather than at the court. This miscarriage of justice may point out the inadequacy of the whole Althing, or it may only signify the system was liable to abuse. As Odd is vindicated in the rest of the saga, we are left to judge. At any rate, Odd is "speechless" at the verdict (ch. 5).

Old Ofeig, whom Odd has basically ignored since his rise to affluence, now comes to his son's aid. Symbolically, the "old" Iceland can help out the new order of commerce and, with it, corruption. Ofeig at first mocks his son to this effect: "How could a great man like you make a mistake in a legal action? I knew there was a flaw but you insist on doing everything yourself and won't take advice." He then points out that "You are better at making money and voyages than at lawsuits" (ch. 5). Odd's disregard for legal technicalities, like his laziness in not attending the court where Ospak continued to exercise his chieftaincy for him, suggests that Icelanders have neglected their civic duty, thereby placing themselves at the mercy of those prepared to use the legal system for unscrupulous ends. Ofeig's shabby appearance symbolizes the neglect of the law and old traditions: "He was wearing a black threadbare coat with only one sleeve left, and the other hanging down his back." The law has become not only ignored, but laughable. However, Ofeig also wears a hood that conceals most of his face — as in "Ale-Hood," this signifies he has something clever, literally, up his sleeve in this case, and that his true identity is yet to be revealed (ch. 5).

Ofeig then asks Odd for a large purse of money, and next begs leave to address the court. He reminds the assembly in an eloquent speech to "judge this case as truthfully and fairly and lawfully as you possibly could" in accordance with the oath that is sworn. If truth, justice, and law come in conflict, as they had in Odd's case, he asks "which is greater?" But the court is not swayed by Ofeig's appeal. The judges' eyes are on the heavy purse of silver he drops from time to time beneath the hem of his coat. Still, he never bribes anyone, but only appears to in order to win his case. The court changes its mind, and Ospak is outlawed (ch. 6).

At Styrmir's instigation, the confederacy of chieftains now forms. Although the pretext is the "shame and humiliation" that Odd has defeated one of their number, Thorarin, and used bribery in court, the eight noblemen are really after Odd's wealth, which would be confiscated — with half to the prosecutors, and half to the people of Odd's quarter of Iceland — were he to be convicted and outlawed for the bribe. Odd, trusting too much to justice, is unperturbed by the plot, but Ofeig tells him he had better come up with a strategy to counter "the most powerful chieftains in the land." Ofeig has Odd give him a great deal of money, and then urges him to appear ready to abscond with all his wealth. When Odd suggests instead that he challenge the suit with his supporters, Ofeig talks him out of it. Common sense justice espoused by Odd is no longer possible; the spirit and intelligence of old Iceland represented by his father must be brought down to modern times to deal with the corruption by subterfuge (ch. 7).

Ofeig's strategy is to approach two of the confederates, wean them away from the group, and then persuade the entire band to accept self-judgment of two of their number whom he chooses. The two would be Egil Skulason and Gellir. The arguments he uses with each tell us much about the strengths and weaknesses of Icelandic society.

Ofeig approaches Egil first. He recites a poem — always a sign of an important point in a saga — that ‘‘My son was a source of pride to me, though he would never let me near his house. But the fool knew nothing of the laws of the land even though he's made a lot of money.’’ He then flatters Egil, calling him a wise man, remarking that Egil has always been most generous to all visitors. That is why Egil is short of money. But by participating in a plot of ‘‘eight greedy men who have justice for sale’’ Egil would not only lose his reputation for wisdom and goodness, but he would get little money. Odd, his father notes, is preparing to leave the country, and all Egil would get is a small share of Odd's land, which wasn't worth much. Ofeig pleads the justice of his son's case: ‘‘No one can rightly call a man an outlaw when such an unjust action is the cause of it; it's his prosecutors who will suffer in the end, and receive only worthless land, disgrace, and humiliation.’’ Ofeig's logic softens Egil up, but his offer of 240 ounces of fine silver wins him over. A bribe is needed to win a case where the accusation is bribery, yet the reader is convinced this is the only way justice can be done. Ofeig exults: ‘‘You want to be chieftains, but you have no idea how to get out of a difficult situation’’ (ch. 8).

Ofeig next turns his attention to Gellir, a proud and noble chieftain who, like Egil, is short of money. In his case, the problem is not excessive generosity, but a large family, especially a daughter for whom he lacks a dowry adequate to entice a worthy husband. Egil and Gellir are sympathetic figures, the most receptive to reason and justice of the eight, for each is only participating because he is in a bad way, having honored his social and familial obligations too well. Ofeig offers Odd as a prospective suitor, and another 240 ounces of silver as the dowry; if Gellir has doubts about Odd's suitability, Ofeig warns that if necessary Odd would come for Gellir's daughter, burn down his house, and leave the country before anyone could do anything. The combination of bribery and threat compels Gellir to see reason (ch. 9).

Ofeig now takes on a wholly new aspect. His eyes twinkle. He lifts his hood and reveals his face. He stands up straight where he had previously pleaded for sympathy by tottering about (ch. 8). The confederates are amazed that he is willing to give two of them self-judgment, but they accept it. Then Ofeig dramatically goes into a tirade, condemning six of his adversaries while offering enough of a mixed judgment on Egil and Gellir so no one suspects their secret arrangement (ch. 10). Styrmir, the group's instigator, was Ofeig's own chief. ''Many a splendid gift I gave you, but you repaid me with evil'' by trying to destroy my son, Ofeig notes. Styrmir also neglected to protect his tenants. Thorarin was the first to try to damage Odd. Hermund, motivated by ''greed and spite'' was the most vehement. Jarnskeggi was so proud of himself he had a banner carried before him like a king, but Ofeig declares: ''You shall not be king in this case.'' The same is true of Broddi, who was praised by the King of Norway as most suited of all Icelanders to be king — another aristocrat with a grossly inflated opinion of himself. Thorgeir had never judged an important case, and had the brains of an ox or an ass. But Gellir, although ''nothing but avarice attracted you to this case,'' had the excuse of a large family to feed — not to mention a daughter to marry off — and Ofeig trusted to the fact that ''he was never before linked with injustice.'' So he is the first arbiter.

Before selecting Egil as his second arbiter, Ofeig delivers a speech on the state of justice in Iceland to make his choices seem genuine. ''Once I could select men with great courage, now I have only the wolf's tail left,'' he laments. But then he turns the metaphor of the wolf on his adversaries: ''The same has happened to me as the wolves; they devour one another, and don't know it till they come to the tail.'' Egil has a reputation of being ''wicked'' and willing to do anything for money. But he never pretended to be otherwise — although Ofeig's previous conversation suggested he was a much better man than that — whereas ''others in this case have been considered just men, though now they've abandoned fairness and justice and become champions of injustice and greed instead'' (ch. 10).

Egil and Gellir now do their work: Egil grins and says, ''this isn't the first time I will acquire honor, even though nobody else wants me to get it.'' Gellir, for the two of them, awards the confederates thirteen ounces of inferior silver, a meaningless sum, for ''the action was started so unjustly.'' He then suggests that little love was lost among the great chieftains, and that in addition to being greedy and corrupt, they frequently quarreled among themselves: ''The worse they fare, the better I'll like it'' (ch. 10). Of course, he and Egil are well-fixed thanks to Ofeig's bribes.

Now it is Egil's turn to insult the stupidity and greed of the six remaining confederates, for the second part of the Althing's ritual was that a judgment had to be defended against those who opposed it. To Hermund's insistence that 130 ounces would have been too little and that Egil was untrustworthy, Egil retorts: "I'm glad I betrayed someone who trusts no one, even himself," and calls attention to Hermund's hiding some buried treasure so well that he himself could never find it. Hermund then insults Egil's poverty, pointing out that it was almost impossible for Hermund to persuade Egil to leave his house after he invited him to visit for Christmas. Only then did Egil return to his "miserable" place to "starve." Egil juxtaposes the truth: "Everybody knows I'm never short of food, although sometimes I'm short of cash." He then turns on Styrmir, who calls him a cheat, by terming Styrmir a coward who runs at the first sign of danger, and a man who has plenty but starves his own household. Egil makes an obscene joke about Thorarin before he can even open his mouth. Thorir is the butt of his servants' mockery. Thorgeir is primarily noted for being beaten by a small farmer and then taking his lambs in compensation. The other confederates, bullies when united, are afraid even to open their mouths for fear their true colors will be revealed to the Althing through Egil's scorn.

At the conclusion of Egil's defense, Ofeig declaims a poem to the Althing, "so that more people can remember this court and the outcome of this case." Like the saga itself, the triumph of justice through intelligence over cowards and bullies who would manipulate the law ought to set a precedent. Ofeig concludes: "Warriors boast of beating weaker foes than mine. I toast my triumph. Poor as I am I proudly say that I fooled these heroes and threw dust in their eyes." The old man, the symbol of a well-run Icelandic republic, has assumed the mantle of the warrior. He is challenging his people that a legal victory consonant with true justice is every bit as honorable, if not more so, than winning a battle, and that the courts are open to everyone with intelligence and courage. He is challenging Icelanders to take back their republic. The subtext is that he was not poor, as he claims. Bribery did the right thing for the wrong reason. Is the saga subtly making the point that bullying and bribing, aristocratic or financial domination, are the only two alternatives, not real justice? The great sympathy with which Ofeig is depicted leads us to hope not, although in his moment of triumph, his son does not talk of justice, but of "hoodwinking" the great, or, as Egil puts it, ''no one has ever taken the wind out of the sails of so many chieftains'' (ch. 10).

Bandamanna Saga concludes with a fairly successful resolution. It is not perfect, realistically signifying that problems will continue to plague Iceland under any government. But it is about as satisfactory as could be hoped for. Odd at first calls his father a ''miserable wretch,'' thinking he has given up the defense, only to be amazed how quickly old Ofeig has won. The overjoyed Odd promises his father will have all the money he wants for the rest of his life in an ideal fusion of the best of the new and old Iceland. But Odd does not remain at home; he is off on another trading voyage, where he proves his ability by rowing off into calm waters with his crew while a Norwegian boat stays behind — Odd has climbed to a mountain and seen a distant wind coming. But he does not go off to Norway, the scene of so many Icelanders' downfall. He heads to Orkney, another land settled by seekers after freedom, and returns with much-needed foodstuffs, ''the best provisions.'' He then honors Gellir and Egil with many ''magnificent'' gifts, and cultivates other ''distinguished'' folk in that way too. Odd has realized it is not enough to make your fortune and go your own way — you need powerful connections. In fact, Odd is reluctant to donate further to Gellir and Egil at first, since Ofeig paid them so well for justice, but the old man advises him to pile the gifts on. Odd now listens to his father's wisdom and gives Gellir sixty sheep and two oxen; he is a different man than the arrogant merchant who ignored his father and started a feud with Ospak over forty sheep (ch. 11).

Ospak, however, returns, to find that his wife, thinking him dead, has married Mar. Ospak kills some of Odd's horses and cows before slaying Mar, at which time he offers the saga's final poem: ''I drew my sharp-edged sword and thrust it deep into Mar's stomach. I could not bear the thought of this man in bed with my lovely Svala.'' In the midst of Odd's triumph, his reconciliation with two of the chieftains and with his father, Ospak comes back to remind us of the price of peace. He too was a hard-working man whose ambition came up against Odd's; whereas Odd could achieve justice and move up the social ladder, Ospak could only reap exile and death. His death at Odd's hands casts a shadow on an otherwise happy ending, which mentions that Odd had many prominent descendants, and lived in peace with his father for the rest of his life (ch. 12).

Ale-Hood's brief tale is similar to *Bandamanna Saga.* Another hooded merchant is first persecuted by and then indicts the great chieftains of Iceland for their injustice at the Althing. Ale-Hood was so known because he made money brewing ale for the Althing and always wore a hood over his face. He was not especially popular: ''Everyone did not like his ale and many did not like him either.'' Once while brewing his ale, Ale-Hood fell asleep and burned not only his own woods but some neighboring trees belonging to Snorri the Priest, Skapti the Law-Speaker, and four other notables. Although the six great men incarnate in themselves the religious and political establishment of Iceland and are very well off, all they can think of is the possibility of a profitable lawsuit.

At first Ale-Hood is his usual disagreeable self. He ''stormed about and threatened and said Skapti would not be boasting'' of the certainty of receiving heavy damages once Ale-Hood's friends appeared at the Althing. But Ale-Hood is out of his league. A small merchant like himself cannot match the clout of Iceland's leading figures, and people not only refuse to help him, but he is shunned and no one even buys his ale (ch. 1).

Ale-Hood now changes his tune. He finally wins the pity of Broddi and Thorstein by transforming himself from a proud fool into a sniveling coward, ''crying his eyes out'' and throwing himself at their feet. They agree to take his case, realizing that it was ''very mean-spirited'' to threaten to outlaw Ale-Hood over a small and not very valuable stand of trees unless he paid a greatly disproportionate fine. Unaware of Ale-Hood's negotiations, Skapti and his group agree to let Broddi and Thorstein arbitrate. Ironically, Ale-Hood still is not receiving justice because anyone believes in it: he has made himself a pitiable, pathetic figure and won some sympathy (ch. 2).

The common man cannot have justice without playing tricks. Like Ofeig, Ale-Hood must demean himself and hide his true identity to have a chance at a fair hearing. But once Broddi and Thorstein are on his side, he stands straight and tall. They award the greedy chiefs less than half the price of a cow among them, six ells of homespun cloth each. In their defense of their judgment, they mince no words, charging the chiefs with ''abusing their power'' and making a huge issue over some trees they had never used and weren't worth very much as an excuse to steal Ale-Hood's money. In the exchange of insults with the chiefs, Broddi also accuses them of having sex with mares and stallions, suggesting bestial, unnatural behavior.

The confederates planned to revenge themselves on Broddi, but one of them, Thorkel, moved by Broddi's mentioning that their fathers were both killed in the same battle, warned him of the plot. The chiefs' ambush drives home how dangerous it was to do justice against the wishes of powerful people at the Althing. But remembering a feud which killed both their fathers, Broddi and Thorkel decide to make peace. When Broddi courageously refuses to change his route home in response to the news, Thorkel agrees to accompany him to deter his erstwhile allies. The tale ends by telling us they lived in friendship for the rest of their lives. Justice could be achieved in Iceland, if men of good will supported it at the Althing and continued to protect each other from those who would take revenge when the law did not suit their wishes. It also helped if they honored the comradeship shared by their fathers. Such a solution to Iceland's ills in the days of the corrupt chieftaincy which led to the republic's destruction may not have been possible, but it was still a standard the sagas could hold up before their fellow citizens. It is a model from which we can still profit.

Chapter Seven

COMMUNITY PROBLEMS: *EYRBYGGJA SAGA*

Synopsis: Unlike the early days of Iceland, when resources were plentiful and chiefs compromised their problems, the pagan Arnkel and the Christian Snorri the Priest head two rival clans. These are spurred on to murder and pitched battles by Arnkel's violent father Thorolf Twist-Foot and Snorri's amorous nephew Gunnlaug. The pagan Arnkel, a man morally superior to the intriguing Christian Snorri, is killed. Snorri survives in an unsettled atmosphere where renewed feuding is always a possibility, and the chiefs must be checked by the community of farmers who wish to keep peace and preserve the republic.

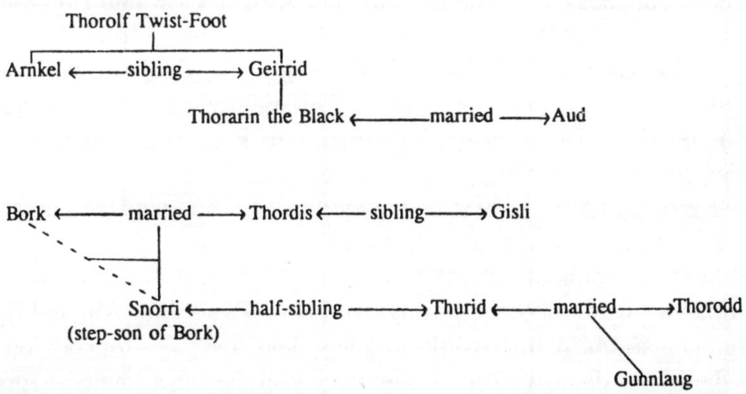

The modern translators of *Eyrbyggja Saga* — the story of the people of the Eyr region in western Iceland — comment that ''the structure of the saga is so complicated that many readers have compared it unfavorably with *Njal's Saga*, *Gisli's Saga*, or *Grettir's Saga*, where the hero's life is so central to the narrative that it provides a clearly defined structural core.''[1] A central figure exists in *Eyrbyggja Saga*, Snorri — the name itself means ''trouble'' — who ''more than anyone else persuaded the people of the west to embrace Christianity'' (ch. 49). But not only does the saga fail to focus as sharply on him as do most sagas on their protagonist, he also has no claim to moral superiority in the complicated world of conflicting religions and codes of conduct which underlie the narrative. He mirrors *Eyrbyggja Saga* in his very multi-faceted, indefinable personality. ''He was unusually calm, and it was hard to tell when he was pleased,'' the author tells us. He is also described as ''very shrewd with unusual foresight, a long memory, and a thirst for vengeance'' — a ''very powerful'' man whom some ''bitterly resented,'' but a wise man who advised his friends well whereas ''his enemies learned to mistrust his counsel'' (ch. 15).

Snorri is morally inferior to the leader of a rival clan, the pagan priest Arnkel, who dies before the arrival of Christianity but has more of a Christian spirit: ''Everyone grieved for Arnkel, the best man of pagan times. He was shrewd, calm, kind, brave, honest, and sincere.'' Like Snorri's manipulative power, his greatness provoked the envy of lesser people: ''He won every lawsuit which explains why people were so jealous of him, which appeared in the violent way he died'' (ch. 37). Neither goodness nor adherence to law, Arnkel's sad fate suggests, were useful survival skills in republican Iceland, the saga implies by juxtaposing Snorri and Arnkel. For it is the enigmatic, duplicitous leader who engineers the precarious fusion of Christianity, family alliances, legal settlements, and consensual agreements to keep something of a social order going.

Eyrbyggja Saga is best understood as a comprehensive compendium of Iceland's endemic social, familial, religious, psychological, and political problems of which the various ghosts and sorcerers who appear in this tale are symbols requiring exorcism. Describing kin and factional alignments almost impossible to keep clear, the saga touches on nearly all the issues dealt with more intensively in the other sagas — problems of the Althing, women, outlaws, inheritances, foreign influences, economic scarcity, etc. — and the diverse peaceful and warlike, legal and informal, Christian and pagan solutions which could deal with them. The fact that this saga is named after the people of a region rather than being ''Snorri's Saga'' is a hint at this interpretation, as is the way in which many other leading sagas and their characters — Njal, Gisli, Gudrun, Eirik the Red, and Grettir — make cameo appearances. If there are heroes in *Eyrbyggja Saga*, they are the ''people of goodwill [who] considered it terrible that great men who were close neighbors remained bitter enemies, good people sympathetic to both sides who tried to end their feud'' (ch. 46). The saga is thus as turbulent and enigmatic as the Icelandic republic itself, yet a tribute to an underlying community of ''good people'' who for all their shortcomings kept alive self-rule and freedom for four centuries while most of Europe was dominated by lords and kings.

Eyrbyggja Saga is typical in that it begins with a prologue, set at the beginning of Iceland's history, ''when there was enough food on both land and sea'' (ch. 4). Here it was possible to solve through law and consensus problems which later prove intractable. In Norway, Thorolf Mostur-Beard and Bjorn stood staunchly together against the tyranny of King Harald Fair-Hair. Thorolf emigrated to Iceland, where he set up a temple and law court: ''It was so holy that he would let no one defile it, either with bloodshed or excrement'' (ch. 4). Bjorn joins him later, after he refuses his kinfolk's offer to remain with them in the Hebrides. They had become Christians, and Bjorn thought them ''weak-minded'' for deserting the faith of their ancestors (ch 5). As with *Njal's Saga* and others, pagan Iceland in its heroic age is held up as a model; Christianity is for the weak, which is how the saga writers, whose pagan sympathies come through, could justify its appropriateness for an Iceland ruled by Norway after 1262.

Thorolf and Bjorn get on, but after their deaths their heirs quarrel. Bjorn's people find it inconvenient to walk some distance to relieve themselves while worshipping; when they ignore the prohibition Thorolf's son bars them from the temple (ch. 9). A bloody battle ensues, but the community of well-intentioned neighbors makes its first appearance. They send for a mediator, Thord Gellir, with close ties to both groups. He reaches a compromise. The temple ground is desacralized, and a new temple is built in which both clans can serve as priests. Whether the problem was the pride of Thorolf's clan or the inability of Bjorn's to be sufficiently devoted to the traditional religion is immaterial — the new solution satisfies everyone at no cost to anyone. Thord also institutes the West Quarter Courts on the site of Thorolf's temple: justice has passed from the private possession of powerful men to the community at large, from feudal to republican government. Marriages between the two families, who pledge to support each other's lawsuits, cement the peace (ch. 10).

One fly mars the ointment. The prologue briefly introduces Thorolf Twist-Foot, a ''great-viking'' but a ''cruel'' man who will appear over and over, both in life and as a ghost, as the principal source of disorder in the Icelandic state and soul. He is the other Thorolf to Thorolf Mostur-Beard, the foot to the head, injustice and rage to justice and peace. Thorolf Twist-Foot's mother, Geirrid, had been "the finest of women" who "built a hall right across the main road" and kept a perpetual table for the refreshment of travelers. She represents the peace, prosperity, and generosity for which Icelanders of the saga-age longed. But with Thorolf, scarcity and meanness has set in. "Thorolf thought his mother had not acquired nearly enough land, so he challenged Ulfar the Champion to single combat for some land that he owned," Ulfar being "old and childless" (ch. 8). Ulfar, representative of traditional Icelandic honor and the founding generation, preferred death with honor to surrender; he fought with Thorolf and was killed. This duel tells us a new spirit is alive in Iceland: the second generation, scornful of the founders' achievement, turns to selfishness, quarreling, and murder.

Snorri the Priest is at the heart of most of the saga's action. His real name was Thorgrim, but his parents call him Snorri which means "Trouble-maker" to describe his nature (ch. 12). He is the priest for an age of Twist-Foots. His first great deed occurs in the middle of a violent family quarrel. His uncle Gisli (of *Gisli's Saga*) had killed his father, at which time his mother Thordis remarried. Young Snorri got on poorly with his step-father Bork. When Snorri was fifteen, Eyjolf, one of Bork's clan, avenged the murder by killing Gisli — Icelanders could bide their time for years. Bork praised Eyjolf for having removed a stain on the family's honor; Thordis, loyal to her brother, responded by dropping a spoon while she was serving Eyjolf and then stabbing him with a sword when she pretended to pick it up. Snorri then protected his mother when Bork tried to beat her. Eyjolf was Thord Gellir's son, which shows how the peace Thord had achieved was broken not only by quarrels between families, but by murderous fights within families, between husband and wife, father and son.

Shortly after, Bork gives Snorri money to take a trip abroad, in the hopes of getting rid of him. But unlike the great Icelandic heroes for whom a trip abroad is a disaster, for the clever Snorri it is the first step in his rise to greatness. He travels as a pauper, saves his money, and buys out, on a dare, his step-father's share of the sacred mountain of Helgafell first consecrated by Thorolf Mostur-Beard. Bork never dreamed the boy possessed such wealth. Snorri is established through his cunning as Thorolf's successor, and he throws Bork out for good measure after his mother divorces him and takes over the estate (ch. 14).

After these family squabbles are temporarily settled, we next get a taste of the sorcery which plagued Iceland. Snorri's nephew Gunnlaug visits Geirrid, the daughter of Thorolf Twist-Foot, to learn witchcraft, and becomes her lover. This arouses the jealousy of Katla, who makes repeated advances to him which he spurns. One night Gunnlaug is seriously injured, "scratched all over his shoulders and his flesh torn to the bone." Katla's son spreads the rumor Geirrid is responsible. Gunnlaug's father Thorbjorn, supported by his brother-in-law Snorri, take the case to the Law Court. But the jury rules her innocent after her brother Arnkel the Priest, her son Thorarin the Black, and others swear on the altar ring that she is innocent, to the anger of the plaintiffs (chs. 15, 16). Jealousy between women, witchcraft, rumors, and what seems to be a loophole in the law start the monumental feud between Snorri and Arnkel.

A quarrel over horses adds fuel to the flame. Thorbjorn and Thorarin both pasture horses in the same place. Thorbjorn accuses Thorarin of stealing his herd, imaginatively interpreting the insight of a local seer, Spa-Gils: "I don't think the horses have gone far, and it's hard to fix the blame." A soothsayer's prophecies are ambiguous, as in many sagas, but people interpret them so as to confirm their suspicions. Thorbjorn then completely ignores Spa-Gils advice that "it's better to accept one's losses than to cause a lot of trouble." Thorbjorn — "who had a high opinion of himself and gave lesser men a hard time" — goes with eleven men to Thorarin's house and insists on searching the premises despite Thorarin's protests that he has not taken the proper legal steps — obtaining witnesses and a warrant. Thorbjorn takes this insistence that the law be observed as an admission of guilt. Taunted as to why he is so upset if he has nothing to hide, Thorarin, "a quiet man who minded his own business," is about to let Thorbjorn have his way when his mother Geirrid repeats a charge frequently made by her son's enemies: "You are more of a woman than a man putting up with Thorbjorn's insults. What did I ever do to deserve a son like you" (ch. 15). Goaded beyond endurance, Thorarin's men attack the search party. The women of the house, led by Aud, Thorarin's wife, try to stop the fight; while they are doing so, Aud's hand is accidentally chopped off which increases their fury. Thorbjorn is killed and his men are defeated. As the quarrel of the two clans progresses, women become involved both as agitators and peacemakers, men's masculinity is challenged, and Thorarin's respect for law is interpreted as proof of his lawlessness.

Realizing Snorri will come after him, either in court to outlaw him or with an armed force, Thorarin seeks support from his uncle Arnkel.

His pleas are filled with reminders of his peaceful disposition. He looks back nostalgically on the past — "I remember the merry times before I dealt Thorbjorn his death-blow"; "The sweet seasons I went sailing are gone forever." He "tried to overcome his bitterness," for "fighting filled him with fear and loathing," but "he only sought justice in the face of slander." He still has "faith in justice," but knows that in Iceland this cannot be obtained on the sheer merits of the case. A successful verdict requires the support of powerful chiefs. Thorarin's moving speech shows how peaceful people who only wish to be left alone can no longer remain apart from the quarrels that have taken over Iceland.

Arnkel agrees to support Thorarin, but before the case is heard, his sister Geirrid tells him that Katla's son Odd had chopped off Aud's hand. Thorarin now has no problem with an illegal search, but is foiled when Katla, who is a witch, successively turns Odd into the distaff she used for spinning, her goat, and her pet hog on the first three searches. Thorarin brings his mother along on the fourth to counteract any magic, finds Odd, hangs him, and has Katla stoned to death. But before she dies, she tells the group that she, not Geirrid, was the cause of Gunnlaug's injuries, and thus "caused all the trouble." She also curses Arnkel, and predicts he will suffer greatly in life from the heritage of his father, Thorolf Twist-Foot (ch. 20).

Snorri takes charge of the lawsuit for Thorbjorn's death. The peaceful Thorarin is trying to flee the country before vengeance can be taken or outlawry pronounced, but Snorri secretly burns his ship. Arnkel buys him another, and he moves to Britain (chs. 22, 25). Thorarin and his men are outlawed *in absentia*, although all he sought was to uphold the law, defend his house, and eliminate an evil sorceress to boot (chs. 22, 25). When they sail to Britain, Snorri confiscates their property. Ironically, Thorarin was indirectly responsible for the loss of Thorbjorn's horses: his aggressive stallion drove the herd into the mountains, where they were killed in a snowstorm (ch. 23). The horses of Thorarin and Thorbjorn reversed their masters' personalities; it seems even animals are becoming involved in the disputes.

Before resuming the narrative of Snorri's rivalry with Arnkel, four auxiliary tales reveal other sources of tension. At the same assembly where Thorarin is outlawed, Illugi the Black sues Tin-Forni, his father-in-law, for his wife's dowry, to which he is entitled but which the old man refuses to surrender. At first Tin-Forni agrees to turn it over, but only because his supporters were prevented from reaching the assembly by the snowstorm. When they arrive, he repudiates the settlement and a battle ensues in which seven people are killed before "Snorri the Priest asked people to calm things down, and arranged a truce." Snorri is more objective and representative of communal good will when he is not a party to the issue at hand. Here argument over a dowry is the *casus belli*, which turns a law court into a brawl for the first time in the saga. Litigants had to show up with as many supporters as possible to win their cases through force, rather than the law. A poet writing about the court noted "Pledged to keep peace, they dishonored their promise," thereby preserving the sad tale of the law's collapse for future remembrance (ch. 17).

Sheep cause the next quarrel. Helgi, Snorri's shepherd, wounds Vigfus, whose wife is Arnkel's niece, in an argument over where the animals can be pastured. Vigfus prosecutes, but his case fails because the court rules he unlawfully assaulted the shepherd even though he was a man of lower rank. Scarcity of land fit for pasture and farming was a major problem in Iceland, and this brief episode symbolizes the fights that broke out between sheepherders (ch. 23).

The third case involves the famous Eirik the Red, founder of Greenland and father of Leif Eiriksson, who killed some men in a fight over timber, yet another scarce commodity. Despite efforts to hide his ship so he could not escape, Eirik does. The tempers of Icelanders are chasing people overseas, not just to Britain and back to Norway, but to new lands where their quarrels continue (ch. 24).

The fourth episode concerns berserks, men who "once they worked themselves up into a frenzy were wholly inhuman, raging about like mad dogs and afraid of nothing," whose presence plagued all the Scandinavian countries. This incident also involves women and the desire for social mobility based on merit. Vermund, an Icelander who "belonged to a distinguished family," made the usual trip to Norway where the king honored him with gifts in return for military service. Most of these journeys ended tragically, through the overweening pride royal favor instilled in its recipients. Vermund insists the king give him his two berserks, for he thinks they will keep his brother Styr from bullying him as he had back in Iceland. The king warns him that "controlling those madmen will be far too much for a farmer's son," but he keeps his promise to reward Vermund as he chose. The berserks, then, play the same game with Vermund: they only agree to accompany him if he would grant all their wishes. One of the two, Hailli, wants a wife, but

Vermund keeps putting him off as "he knew of no honorable woman who would want to deal with a berserk." Just as Vermund sought to elevate his status — quite low in Iceland thanks to his overbearing brother — by the trip to Norway, the berserk is hoping to gain respectability in Iceland. Vermund ultimately tricks his brother into taking the berserks off his hands, whereupon Hailli falls in love with Styr's daughter. After a meeting with Snorri, Styr sets Hailli a variety of tasks "to compensate for your poverty" to win his daughter. Then, when the berserks are worn out from the hard work, Styr traps them in a bath house, kills them, and marries his daughter to Snorri (ch. 28). The only people to emerge with credit in this incident are the wise king of Norway and the unfortunate berserks, who only want the same status and love as other people. A monarch and his slaves prove superior to freemen.

The main quarrel between Snorri and Arnkel resumes thanks to old Thorolf Twist-Foot; "the older he got, the more violent he became" (ch. 30). First he orders his henchmen to steal some hay from a hardworking farmer named Ulfar, whose advice on haymaking he had ignored which caused his hay to be ruined. When his just son Arknel slaughters some oxen to compensate Ulfar with food, Thorolf promises six of his slaves their freedom to burn Ulfar to death in his house. Arnkel catches and kills them (ch. 31), and assumes legal protection of Ulfar and his land. Thorolf then gets Snorri to join with him against his son Arnkel, descending to accompanying Snorri to court in a lawsuit over Arnkel's killing the slaves. Thorolf is not motivated by financial gain — he promises Snorri the best woodland in the district for his help, an illegal act as it is unlawful to bribe someone to take a case — but by sheer cantankerousness and pride at not being able to get his way in everything. Here hay and wood, two scarce resources, combine with rich and powerful men riding roughshod over the rights of a poor, honest farmer to form the substance of the quarrel.

At the Althing, Arnkel argues that arsonists can be legally killed. Snorri counters that this is only so if they were killed in self-defense on the spot, whereas Arnkel took them away and hanged them. Snorri wins a judgment of twelve ounces of silver per slave, after "people stepped in to make peace." But Thorolf is not satisfied with a fairly generous judgment for the slaves. "I never dreamed you'd be so slack in taking the case," he tells Snorri, and even thinks his son would have given him a better deal with a self-judgment. Thorolf soon returns to his friend, the sorcerer Spa-Gils, and in his wrath tosses their relationship aside. He gives the poor man the choice of paying three ounces of silver he owes or killing Arnkel. A free man is bribed to do murder like a slave, and to murder a man's own son at that. Arnkel's men catch and kill Spa-Gils. Snorri criticizes Arnkel: "He tramples on everybody in this neighborhood," and promises that "the stronger" — meaning himself — "is sure to win" (chs. 31, 32). Snorri has repudiated peacemaking and justice; his use of the courts is now seen purely as a tactic in the feud rather than a means of resolving it.

But Snorri also quarrels with Thorolf Twist-Foot. The old scoundrel complains that Snorri is ruining the woods the saga leads us to believe he gave Snorri, although Thorolf now claims he only gave him the right to fell some trees. Thorolf now goes back to Arnkel and suggests they unite again against Snorri. Arnkel is the true man of peace: "I know he has no legal rights to [the forest], but I won't have you and your ugly temper gloating over a quarrel between me and Snorri." Thorolf calls his son a coward, storms off in a rage, and is found stone dead in his high seat the next morning. His grim countenance left everyone numb with terror, and it was almost impossible to bury him and move the corpse (ch. 33).

Thorolf is as stubborn and evil as a ghost as he was while alive. He has to be reburied twice: demons kill the oxen which are needed to haul him off. Beasts which approached his grave "lost their minds and howled themselves to death." Sheep, birds, and shepherds in the neighborhood died of fright. Thorolf even haunted his widow: "She was driven insane, and the strain of it killed her." Arnkel finally reburies his father at an "uncorrupted spot." His ghost rests — while Arnkel lives (ch. 34).

But even Arnkel cannot settle the disputes with Snorri his father stirred up. Snorri and Arnkel still argue over the rights to the woods. Snorri's friend Hauk is killed by Arnkel's shepherd while using them. Since Hauk's assault, like that on Vigfus, is unprovoked, Arnkel wins a lawsuit which follows. Then it is rumored Snorri is sending people to kill Arnkel. None succeed, but the following year Snorri's childhood companion, Thorleif Kimbi, angered that Arnkel has won compensation for all the people killed in his household by Snorri's folk, leads a party and slays Arnkel while he is making hay. Arnkel has slaves working with him, but they will not help him — Arnkel worked every day from morning to night and demanded the same of his bondsmen. Here is a sudden, unexpected perspective on Arnkel — the great champion of justice among his equals and Iceland's free people is detested by his own slaves whom he exploits unmercifully (ch. 37.)

Arnkel's legal heirs were all women, and because of Snorri's power and influence no one will help them prosecute the murder. Their efforts are feeble — the only one punished is Thorleif Kimbi, who is outlawed for three years. The community, however intimidated by Snorri for his particular interest in this case, still passes a law that neither a man under age sixteen nor a woman be permitted to prosecute a manslaughter again. The next of kin, whomever he might be, would be obliged to take up this duty. While barred from the courts, women and children could not be kept apart from the battles of their men (ch. 38).

Even outlawry, which was supposed to remove a person especially likely to provoke a quarrel from Iceland, fails to work, for the feuds spread overseas. Thorleif Kimbi is leaving on the same ship as Arinbjorn of Arnkel's family, who is on his way to Norway to search for his brother Bjorn. Bjorn too had been outlawed for killing two of Snorri's retainers — they had tried to revenge Snorri's half-sister Thurid with whom Bjorn had committed adultery (ch. 19). On the voyage, Thorleif and Arinbjorn fight over cooking porridge for the crew, which in the absence of women every man takes his turn doing. Just as women become involved in men's quarrels, so deep is the resentment between the clans that men are fighting over women's issues. Thorleif spills Arinbjorn's porridge as a sign of contempt, for which the latter hits him on the neck with a hot ladle, permanently scarring him. It takes the Norwegian majority of the crew to make peace between them, an ironic reversal of how Iceland was originally founded as a republic of laws to end the feuding endemic to the Norwegian monarchy and aristocracy. Faced with Norwegian scorn, Thorleif talks Arinbjorn into patching up their differences — for the moment: "It wouldn't be right to give the Norwegians a chance to make fun of us, and separate us like a pair of fighting dogs." But he promises to get even when they return to Iceland (ch. 39). The implication is even Norwegian control, established by the time *Eyrbyggja Saga* was written, cannot bring about real peace on the troubled island.

Indeed, if anything the vendetta grows fiercer when the men come back to Iceland in three years. Bjorn resumes his Romeo and Juliet type of romance with Snorri's half-sister Thurid. While doing so he sings some eloquent songs which express his loneliness and how the arranged marriages many prominent Icelanders were forced into by their families led to such situations. Thurid's husband Thorodd hires Thorgrima Witch-Face, a sorceress, to raise a blizzard and prevent Bjorn's visits (ch. 40). Thorleif Kimbi is in a similar situation; he loves a relative of Arnbjorn but cannot marry her because the relationship between the clans prevents it. Then Snorri's and Arnkel's supporters fight at a turf game while the leaders, Snorri and Steinthor of Eyr, who has succeeded Arnkel and shares his benign temperament, are off trying to negotiate a peace (ch. 41). The feud prevents love from being fulfilled and has reached the point where leaders can no longer control their men.

Thorodd and Thorleif Kimbi try to murder Arinbjorn, but the attempt fails. So they try to involve a slave, Egil — not the hero of *Egil's Saga* — "a huge, powerful man who did not like being a slave" (ch. 43) to perform the deed they could not, and promise him his freedom to kill Bjorn, Arinbjorn, or any male member of the clan. The saga's author notes the popular belief that Snorri was behind the whole plot without endorsing it, although strong circumstantial evidence implicates him. This would mean his efforts to make peace earlier, unlike Steinthor's, were mere pretenses. But Egil is killed by Bjorn instead (ch. 43).

Egil's death provokes two major battles, the culmination of the feuds. The struggle between Snorri's and Arnkel's/Steinthor's factions has taken symbolic forms which show how it has degraded the participants and distorted the social order. Men have fought over porridge; now Iceland's greatest families go to war over compensation for a slave. Steinthor, "one of Iceland's three best fighters" but "normally a very quiet man" (ch. 12), was willing to ride to Snorri's house with a small band and pay compensation for Egil, regardless of who was guilty, simply to keep the peace. But Bjorn smells trouble and insists on accompanying him with nearly sixty men. Similarly, Snorri tells his assembled kinsmen and retainers, some eighty in all, that "we must neither bar them from our estate nor refuse Steinthor his legal rights, for he'll do his business quietly and sensibly." But as Steinthor is paying the money with both sides looking on, one of Snorri's women comments: "That Steinthor is a splendid-looking fellow. He also speaks very well" (ch. 44). This remark sets off Thorleif Kimbi and his brothers and the battle is joined. A woman's intervention recalls Thorleif's, Thorodd's and the other participants' frustrated sexual desires, as well as the man's code not to be unmanly in front of women. The battle brings to a head many of the tensions in the book. It is caused by the death of an exploited, freedom-loving slave manipulated by his cowardly owners, and fueled by family rivalry and frustrated love.

But bottom has not yet been reached. During the battle Snorri's twelve-year-old grandson is wounded. It turns out the boy's other grandfather is fighting on Steinthor's side, which caused Snorri to point out the wound, call the man a traitor, and persuade him to change sides. Things have come to such a pass that children are fighting and people are battling their own grandchildren. The usual mediators, the people of the neighborhood, then arrive. They persuade Snorri and Steinthor to make the peace, but now it is Steinthor's pent-up fury which breaks out. He strikes Snorri instead of taking his hand. Snorri's men promise to fight until the last man, but Snorri restrains them and agrees to forego vengeance on Steinthor. But the best peace he can get is a truce with nothing settled and everyone returning home (ch. 44).

A second battle, fought on the ice that winter, follows. Snorri's people are defeated, and most of his blood-brothers wounded. They would have been killed had they not slipped on the ice and Steinthor declared it was dishonorable to fight men who were flat on their backs (ch. 45). The people of the community, outraged at the enmity of such "great and close" neighbors, intervened: Iceland's chiefs and leaders needed to be taught how to govern by less prominent folk. They insisted all outstanding injuries and claims for compensation be evened out and no further revenge taken. Snorri and Steinthor agreed, and the peace was kept as long as they lived (ch. 46).

The only remaining problem was that Bjorn could not keep away from Thurid. Snorri tries to ambush him, but he makes a daring move which not only saves his life but ends this quarrel as well. Bjorn walks right up to Snorri in the midst of his men before they could act and holds a knife to his chest as he appears to greet his pursuers. Snorri agrees to spare Bjorn's life if Bjorn will reciprocate, but insists that "you stop visiting my sister Thurid." Bjorn leaves the country, and the saga states it is probable that he went to the New World. His last known act was to save an Icelander blown off course there from people who appeared to be speaking Irish. (ch. 64). Of other participants in the battles, Thorleif Kimbi joins Eirik in Greenland; another son of Thorbjorn winds up in the New World with Thorfinn Karlsefni (ch. 48). An overpopulated and contentious Iceland can only lessen, not solve, its problems by sending people overseas, where, as *Eirik's* and *Groenlandinga Sagas* show, the feuds continue.

At this point Christianity comes to Iceland, largely through Snorri's efforts (ch. 49). To state the obvious, we never see Snorri "the Priest" engaged in religious rather than political activity, which provides the opportunity to test the effects of conversion on Icelandic society and morality. It doesn't appear to help, for the women next take up the slack and institute fresh imbroglios. Snorri's sister Thurid is again the instigator. A wealthy woman from the Hebrides named Thorgunna comes to Iceland and moves in with Thurid. In addition to possessing an elegant wardrobe, she is extremely religious, attends mass each day, and works at the farm with the strength of a man. She quarrels with Thorgrima Witch-Face, and in this symbolic struggle of the two religions the old pagan rites are more powerful. The skies shower blood on Thorgunna, she sickens and dies. On her deathbed she gives Thurid her scarlet cloak, but asks that her fancy bed-furnishings be burned. Thurid covets them too much to keep her promise to do so (ch. 51). Shortly thereafter ill omens appear, many people die, including Thurid's husband, Thorgrima, and her husband, all of whom haunt the area. Snorri only quiets the ghosts by summoning them to a door-court after the bed furnishings are burned. It requires an elaborate combination of Icelandic legal practice — the door court — with Christian prayers, to get rid of the ghosts. "I stayed as long as you let me" and "There's no peace here" are the spirits' parting words. They are warning that they are not the real cause of the problem, and that things will not improve once they have departed (ch. 50).

The greatest battle of all occurs in the aftermath of the murder of Snorri's father-in-law Styr. He is killed for seducing a farmer's daughter: his ghost has his arms around the girl when Snorri comes to retrieve the body. It falls to Illugi the Black to revenge her — we remember him as the man Snorri had earlier supported to retrieve his dowry, after which he not only arranged a peace with Illugi's father-in-law but refused to take a fee (ch. 17). Such respect for the law is long gone. Snorri, now joined by the men of Eyr led by Steinthor, takes four hundred men to support him in court. Illugi has five hundred, indicating the consolidation of Iceland into ever larger and more deadly coalitions of powerful chiefs as the republic approached its end. Thorstein Gislason, a powerful supporter of Illugi, uses force to forbid Snorri's case over Styr. Snorri is outnumbered, but takes his men home and arranges for Thorstein's murder the following year. Then it is Snorri's turn, as the more powerful party, to bar an action over Thorstein. The Things have ceased to function. When more of Illugi's followers show up and the sides are comparable, a battle breaks out between hundreds of men — the law is now a scene of battle and is being murdered as in *Njal's Saga*, and all to defend the honor of a lecherous old aristocrat who seduced a young woman. As in *Njal's Saga*, an ever-descending spiral of dishonorable, incredible deeds discredits Iceland's ruling class, justifying the eventual Norwegian takeover while simultaneously evoking nostalgia for a properly functioning republic (ch. 56).

Once more, the people of the community step between the factions and arrange a truce. Snorri agrees to the exile of those of his supporters who killed Thorstein Gislason to prevent a hearing at the next Althing, where he had a chance of suffering punishment himself (ch. 56). As with the opening story of the temple of Thorolf Mostur-Beard, both sides will henceforth grant each other free access to the courts, just as they once agreed to share the courts and temples. But the peace so easily achieved when Iceland was founded is now the peace of exhaustion after a long chain of machinations and death.

In an effort to cool things down, Snorri himself switches houses with Gudrun of *Laxdaela Saga* (ch. 56). However, exchanging regions only trades problems. New sources of trouble arise from Ospak, "a great bully" who traveled with a gang of vagabonds who stole food and supplies from the farmers in a time of famine (chs. 57, 58). Snorri had them sentenced to outlawry. He then returned to the district and killed or dispersed them. For all his faults, the Eyr region needed Snorri to protect it against such menaces to order, although a case could be made the aristocrats' struggles were far more pernicious than the devastation caused by a handful of outlaws. Snorri even recognized that they, too, were only trying to survive, for he let Ospak's widow and child live on his farm (ch. 59). But no sooner are the outlaws out of the way than old Thorolf Twist-Foot's ghost reappears, this time as a bull. He was so fearsome that "everyone thought that unless he were eliminated, Thorolf would not stop until he had cleared the region of both men and beasts." Thorolf's corpse was again disinterred. It was still intact, but as large as an ox, with a ferocious aspect. Thorolf and his ghost, like the evils of the district, and indirectly those of the Iceland he had come to symbolize, had grown enormously after his death. He was finally burned (ch. 63).

But the saga comes to an unsatisfactory and inconclusive end. Snorri returned to his new home to farm for twenty years, where he continued to have trouble on his hands from the powerful men of the region. If he became more popular as he aged, it was not because he became juster or less devious, but because his enemies were dying off and ''he entered into many marriage alliances with important people'' (ch. 65). The saga ends with the list of Snorri's prominent descendants and the burial of all the bones from his clan, first at the church he built, and then at a new edifice. Only death ended the feuding.

In *Eyrbyggja Saga*, there is no resolution of the Icelandic republic's degeneration into vicious, civil warfare and aristocratic domination. Things simply get worse and worse, with every conceivable cause of the feuds being aired: men fighting like women over porridge, slaves being hired to kill lords, berserks shaming their masters, courts degenerating into pitched battles. *Eyrbyggja Saga* is both a lament for the just society presented briefly in the saga's prologue and ''good riddance'' to the sorry wreck it became. It is less ambiguous about the republic's faults and more silent on its virtues than any other saga, but as a concentrated account of how any occasion or issue can symbolize and set off fundamental social antagonisms, *Eyrbyggja Saga* is perhaps the finest, most comprehensive account of the reasons Iceland succumbed to monarchy.

Chapter Eight

EPILOGUE: ON THE BEST FORM OF GOVERNMENT AND THE PERSISTENCE OF REPUBLICS

Until liberalism and democracy triumphed in the Western world in the nineteenth century, most European political theory was a variation on the theme of mixed government propounded in Book IV of Aristotle's *Politics*. Monarchy was perhaps the best unmixed government — on those rare occasions when a just and able ruler could be found. Otherwise it degenerated into tyranny. Aristocracy, rule by the best, was rarely that. It was usually a euphemism for government by the wealthy or by hereditary descent. Democracy had the advantage of at least *intending* the good of the majority, but when the majority was the poor, as in most instances, it led to anarchy through efforts to plunder the rich. And anarchy usually ended up in tyranny. With monarchy, aristocracy, and democracy checking each other, the strengths of each could be brought into play while the other two elements watched for signs of a thirst for power or corruption.

Iceland of the sagas was a mixed government. Monarchy was represented, if weakly, by the Law-Speaker, the republic's only paid official. People respected his judgment as to what the law was, unless, as in *Njal's Saga* and *Grettir's Saga*, he undermined his office by pursuing personal gain or misinterpreting the law. Aristocracy appeared through the influence of chiefs. All free men had to attach themselves to a chief; they mutually supported each other both at the Althing and in battle. In *Eyrbyggja Saga* the community controlled the chiefs' vendettas, and Egil worked out a just settlement at the Althing. But in *Njal's Saga* and the *Laxdaela Saga*, symbolizing Iceland in decline, the people's commitment to the chiefs outweighed loyalty to Iceland's system of legal institutions. The Althing, where every man could vote on laws and serve on juries, embodied Iceland's democracy, its dominant element until it degenerated into aristocratic feuding which in turn was replaced by the Norwegian monarchy.

Iceland's mix of the three elements, like that of the United States, was within a republican frame. From ancient Greece to the nineteenth century, political theorists agreed what sort of society produced a stable republic. It had to be small, without great extremes of wealth among its citizens, and preferably agrarian to avoid the class divisions that would arise from commerce. Sparta and Rome, before it was corrupted by imperial ambitions, were ideal republics for the ancient world. The Founding Fathers of the United States used them as exemplars and sang their praises, whence the United States Senate and the classical architecture of Washington, D.C.

Republican theory, from ancient times to the nineteenth century, also stressed that republics should be homogeneous nations of men fit to bear arms.[1] Retaining military sharpness against external enemies reduced quarreling at home. It required the virtue of patriotism and a refusal to become decadent and acquire excessive wealth. Iceland should have been an ideal republic. It was small, rural, homogeneous, and had plenty of martial energy. Unfortunately, it had no enemies. The vikings on the European continent did not relish a fight with the fierce inhabitants of an island with almost no material resources. Many Icelanders, starved for riches and glory, went to the other nations of Scandinavia and fought for their kings. Even this outlet could not tame the people of an increasingly poor and overcrowded island, who fell to fighting among themselves. But it took four centuries for Iceland to end up where most of the world had been all along — subject to a monarch who is almost always depicted as an arbitrary tyrant in the sagas. Until then, Icelanders held fast to their representative institutions.

Theorists, from Romans such as Cicero, Cato, and Tacitus, to Machiavelli in the Italian Renaissance, and the American Founding Fathers, insisted that a republic only survived when its inhabitants retained their virtue — that is, disinterested love of their country and its laws. Corrupted republics, where extremes of wealth and poverty became too great, destroyed themselves through internal factionalism, and ultimately were reduced to tyranny. Only when the framers of the United States Constitution recognized that a large variety of factions in an extensive republic would neutralize each other and prevent a majority, or less likely, a minority, from dominating the rest, did the modern idea of a republic founded on self-interest take shape. Liberty was transformed from the ability of a virtuous population to govern itself to the civil liberties of individuals permitted to do as they pleased if they harmed no one else. And even the American Framers, and their successors up to the present, have periodically reminded the nation that a strong dose of respect for the laws and love of country is still needed.[2] As Abraham Lincoln warned his listeners at the Springfield, Illinois, Lyceum in 1838, Americans who followed the Framers would also crave the opportunity to distinguish themselves in the field of politics. Here lay the danger: tinkering with the republic's institutions. As an antidote, Lincoln urged Americans to acquire "a reverence for the constitution and the laws. . . . Let it become the political religion of the nation; and let the old and the young, the rich and the poor, the grave and the gay, of all sexes and tongues, sacrifice unceasingly upon its altars."[3]

Over five hundred years before Lincoln, a saga writer had Njal say: "Our land will be formed with laws but destroyed through lawlessness" (ch. 70). Njal, who more than any other man in Iceland symbolized and revered the law, suffered a horrible death that signified his nation's destruction. The Icelandic republic previously worked well, even when economic scarcity set in after a few generations, precisely because its inhabitants — some five thousand free farmers and their households — had respected the law which outlawed troublemakers and avoided arbitrary justice in difficult cases by paying compensation to injured parties and their kin. But by the late twelfth and early thirteenth century, the concentration of wealth and power in the hands of a few chieftains and the church led to incessant feuding, pitched battles involving hundreds of men, and the irrelevance of a corrupted system of courts. Increasing dependence on Norway for food and timber combined with the extreme maldistribution of wealth and power led to Norwegian and clerical domination. Iceland did not regain its independence until 1944, during a war that raged across the world.

The so-called family sagas discussed in this book compress Iceland's founding, crisis, and dissolution into the span of a few generations. Written between 1230 (*Egil's Saga*) and the beginning of the fourteenth century, they reveal, as the medieval scholar W.P. Ker wrote, a people "more clearly conscious of their own aims, more critical of their own achievement, than any polity on earth since the fall of Athens."[4] Like Polybius, Tacitus, Machiavelli, Hume, and Montesquieu, they glorify a golden republican age, all the while reflecting profoundly on why it could not last forever.

The wonder of the Icelandic republic is not that it ended, but that it lasted as long as it did. Except maybe Switzerland and San Marino, the world's republics today are young. The United States, the oldest, has endured just over two hundred years. Most date from the twentieth century and have been plagued with dictatorship, revolution, and different kinds of corruption. Iceland's achievement is especially remarkable when we realize its law had to tame the tempers of vikings like Egil and turn them into peaceful farmers; the sagas reveal the community's continuous struggle to make people submit to the legal system rather than take vengeance into their own hands.

For nearly three hundred years, Iceland's struggle was about as successful as any fair observer could reasonably expect. Reverence for the law was so pronounced that it could be enforced consensually by the landholders, without an army or any coercive authority. Sir Walter Scott noted this in his study of *Eyrbyggja Saga*, where he pointed out that even the dead were forced to respect the law as a symbol of the reverence in which it was held. He cited this saga's legal exorcism of the evil spirits: ''All the solemn rites of judicial procedure were observed on this singular occasion. . . . It is the only instance in which the ordinary administration of justice has been supposed to extend over the inhabitants of another world.''[5]

One similar case does come to mind: the trial of Orestes by the people of Athens in Aeschylus' *Oresteia*. Here, eye-for-eye vengeance, symbolized by the Furies, gives way to respect for legal procedures in a just republic. Justice is taken from the harsh, supernatural Furies, who are transformed into the kind ''Eumenides,'' guardians of an Athens committed to fair legal procedures. Iceland, too, tamed the furies for a length rarely equalled in human history.

In addition to the example of its republic, Iceland also gave us the gift of its sagas. Like the works of Thucydides and Euripides, these were the product of maturity resulting from the destruction of a society proud of its special freedom and institutions. Its collapse led to a meditation which equalled the Greek philosophical and dramatic inquiry into the reasons for the persistence and decline of republics. The Icelanders may be compared with the Greeks because, unlike most of the Romans and their Renaissance disciples, they probed their subject from several perspectives, painting a canvas as complicated and vast as the reality they described, looking at the weaknesses as well as the strengths of their republic and the alternatives to it which emerged — monarchy and the Roman church — rather than simply singing its praises and mourning its corruption. If Iceland could not withstand forever the pressures of scarcity, internal war, and dependence on Norway and the Catholic Church, it wrested through literature a final triumph from its tragedy. Never did a perishing republic, to paraphrase Robinson Jeffers, shine more brightly.

Notes

NOTES TO *PREFACE*

1. W. P. Ker, *Epic and Romance: Essays on Medieval Literature* (New York: Dover, 1957; reprint of 1896 edition), pp. 200-201.

2. *Ibid.*; Theodore M. Andersson, *The Icelandic Family Saga: An Analytical Reading* (Cambridge, Mass.: Harvard University Press, 1967); Carol J. Clover, "Icelandic Family Sagas," in *Old Norse-Icelandic Literature: A Critical Guide*, Carol J. Clover and John Lindow, eds., *Islandica* 45 (Ithaca, N.Y.: Cornell University Press, 1985), pp. 239-315; Jesse L. Byock, *Medieval Iceland: Society, Sagas, and Power* and *Feud in the Icelandic Saga* (Berkeley: University of California Press, 1988); the introductions to the saga translations in the Penguin Classics series (cited in the "Notes on Translations and Spelling") by Hermann Pálsson, Magnus Magnusson, and Paul Edwards; Lars Lönnroth, *Njal's Saga: A Critical Introduction* (Berkeley: University of California Press, 1976); Einar Sveinsson, *Njal's Saga: A Literary Masterpiece*, trans. Paul Schach (Lincoln, Neb.: University of Nebraska Press, 1971); Richard F. Allen, *Fire and Iron: Critical Approaches to Njal's Saga* (Pittsburgh: University of Pittsburgh Press, 1971); Paul Schach, *Icelandic Sagas* (Boston: Twayne Publishers, 1984); William Ian Miller, *Bloodtaking and Peacemaking: Feud, Law, and Society in Saga Iceland* (Chicago: University of Chicago Press, 1990); see also the special issue of *Scandinavian Studies* on the sagas, Theodore M. Andersson, ed., 60 (1988).

NOTES TO CHAPTER ONE: *INTRODUCTION*

1. Good accounts of the social and institutional background of the sagas include Jesse L. Byock, *Medieval Iceland: Society, Sagas, and Power* (Berkeley: University of California Press, 1988), and "Governmental Order in Early Medieval Iceland," *Viator* 17 (1986), pp. 19-34; William Ian Miller, *Bloodtaking and Peacemaking: Feud, Law, and Society in Saga Iceland* (Chicago: University of Chicago Press, 1990).

2. Carol J. Clover, "The Politics of Scarcity: Notes on the Sex Ratio in Early Scandinavia," *Scandinavian Studies* 60 (1988), pp. 147-188; "Regardless of Sex: Men, Women, and Power in Northern Europe," *Speculum* 68 (1993), pp. 363-388; Jenny M. Jochens, "The Medieval Icelandic Heroine: Fact or Fiction?", *Viator* 17 (1986), pp. 35-50.

3. Carol J. Clover, ''Icelandic Family Sagas,'' in *Old Norse-Icelandic Literature: A Critical Guide*, Carol J. Clover and John Lindow, eds., *Islandica* 45 (Ithaca, N.Y.: Cornell University Press, 1985), pp. 239-315, esp. p. 269. See also Paul Schach, *Icelandic Sagas* (Boston: Twayne Publishers, 1984), esp. p. 119.

4. Theodore M. Andersson, *The Icelandic Family Saga: An Analytical Reading* (Cambridge, Mass.: Harvard University Press, 1967), esp. ch. l.

5. See Roberta Kevelson, *The Law as a System of Signs* (New York: Plenum Press, 1988) for a seminal work on legal semiotics of much value to me, and Lawrence M. Friedman, *The Legal System* (New York: Russell Sage Foundation, 1975).

6. A good introduction to the subject is Jeffrie Murphy and Jules Coleman, *The Philosophy of Law: An Introduction to Jurisprudence* (Totowa, N.J.: Rowman & Allenheld, 1984).

7. St. Thomas Aquinas, ''The Essence of Law,'' in *Introduction to St. Thomas Aquinas*, Anton C. Pegis, ed. (New York: Random House, 1948), p. 649; C. S. Lewis, *The Abolition of Man* (New York: Macmillan, 1943).

8. John Austin, *The Province of Jurisprudence*, ed. H. L. A. Hart (London: Weidenfeld and Nicolson, 1954; orginally published 1832); H. L. A. Hart, *The Concept of Law* (Oxford: Oxford University Press, 1961).

9. Ronald Dworkin, *Taking Rights Seriously* (Cambridge, Mass.: Harvard University Press, 1977).

10. Edmund Burke, *Reflections on the Revolution in France*, ed. Thomas H. D. Mahoney (New York: Liberal Arts Press, 1955; originally published 1791), p. 71.

11. John Stuart Mill, *Utilitarianism* (London: J. M. Dent, 1910; originally published 1862).

12. Burke, *Reflections*, is the classic work, but he, like Mill, is sensitive to the need to incorporate natural law for society to persist.

13. Jerome Frank, *Law and the Modern Mind* (New York: Brentano's, 1930); Lon L. Fuller, ''American Legal Realism,'' *University of Pennsylvania Law Review* 82 (1934), pp. 429-461.

NOTES TO CHAPTER TWO: *THE HERO AND THE SAGE: NJAL'S SAGA*

1. Lars Lönnroth, *Njal's Saga: A Critical Introduction* (Berkeley: University of California Press, 1976), pp. 165-166.

2. This controversy is discussed in *ibid.*, pp. 17, 181; Magnus Magnusson and Hermann Pálsson, introduction to translation of *Njal's Saga* (Baltimore: Penguin Books, 1960), p. 24; and Einar Sveinsson, *Njal's Saga: A Literary Masterpiece*, trans. by Paul Schach (Lincoln, Neb.: University of Nebraska Press, 1971), p. 39.

3. Lönnroth, *Njal's Saga*, pp. 174-187.

4. Sveinsson, *Njal's Saga*, pp. 43-44.

5. Gwyn Jones, *The Norse Atlantic Saga* (London: Oxford University Press, 1964), pp. 17-19.

6. Christianity came to Iceland In 1000 A. D.; Njal was burned at the the age of eighty, ten years later. See chronology in Magnusson and Pálsson, *Njal's Saga*, p. 375.

7. Lönnroth, *Njal's Saga*, pp. 184, 188-194.

NOTE TO CHAPTER FOUR: *EXCEPTIONAL WOMEN: LAXDAELA SAGA*

1. Carol J. Clover, ''Icelandic Family Sagas,'' in *Old Norse-Icelandic Literature: A Critical Guide*, Carol J. Clover and John Lindow, eds., *Islandica* 45 (Ithaca, N.Y.: Cornell University Press, 1985), pp. 239-315, esp. p. 269. See also Paul Schach, *Icelandic Sagas* (Boston: Twayne Publishers, 1984), esp. p. 119.

NOTE TO CHAPTER SEVEN: *COMMUNITY PROBLEMS: EYRBYGGJA SAGA*

1. Hermann Pálsson and Paul Edwards, introduction to *Eyrbyggja Saga* (London: Penguin Books, 1989), p. 3.

NOTES TO CHAPTER EIGHT: *EPILOGUE*

1. An exhaustive study of the social basis of republics as envisioned by theorists ancient and modern is Paul Rahe, *Republics: Ancient and Modern Classical Republicanism and the American Revolution* (Chapel Hill, N.C.: University of North Carolina Press, 1992); Rahe notes the ancient emphasis on military virtue. For the benefits of an agrarian society and the corrupting potential of commerce in Western thought, see esp. J. G. A. Pocock, *The Machiavellian Moment: Florentine Political Thought and the Atlantic Republican Tradition* (Princeton: Princeton University Press, 1975).

2. See the classic articles by Douglass Adair, ''Experience Must Be Our Only Guide: History, Democratic Theory, and the United States Constitution,'' in Ray Allen Billington, ed., *The Reinterpretation of Early American History: Essays in Honor of John Edwin Pomfret* (San Marino, Cal.: The Huntington Library, 1966), pp. 129-148, and ''That Politics May Be Reduced to a Science: David Hume, James Madison, and the Tenth Federalist,'' *Huntington Library Quarterly* 20 (1957), pp. 343-360.

3. *The Collected Works of Abraham Lincoln*, Roy P. Basler, ed. (New Brunswick, N.J.: Rutgers University Press, 1953), vol. 1, p. 122.

4. W. P. Ker, *The Dark Ages* (New York: Mentor Books, 1958; reprint of 1904 edition), pp. 200-201.

5. Sir Walter Scott, ''Abstract of the *Eyrbyggia-Saga*,'' in Henry Weber and Robert Jamieson, eds., *Illustrations of Northern Antiquities* (London and Edinburgh, 1814), pp. 475-513, quotation from pp. 508-509.

NOTES ON TRANSLATIONS AND SPELLING

In my citations I have compared various modern English translations of the sagas to arrive at a rendering as clear and straightforward as possible for readers of late twentieth-century English. I have rendered the Icelandic letter pronounced "ya" consistently as "j" rather than "i"; þ is represented by "th."

Njal's Saga

Trans. Sir George Webbe Dasent (London: Norroena Anglo-Saxon Classics, 1907).

Trans. Carl F. Bayerschmidt and Lee M. Hollander (New York: American Scandinavian Foundation, 1955).

Trans. Magnus Magnusson and Hermann Pálsson (Baltimore: Penguin Books, 1960).

Grettir's Saga

Trans. Eirik Magnusson and William Morris (London: Longmans, Green, 1900).

Trans. G. A. Hight (London: J. M. Dent, 1929).

Trans. Denton Fox and Herman Pálsson (Toronto: University of Toronto Press, 1974).

Laxdaela Saga

Trans. Thorstein Veblen (New York: B. W. Huebsch, 1925).

Trans. Peter Foote (London: J. M. Dent, 1964).

Trans. Magnus Magnusson and Hermann Pálsson (London: Penguin Books, 1969).

Egil's Saga

Trans. Christine Fell (London: J. M. Dent, 1975).

Trans. Hermann Pálsson and Paul Edwards (London: Penguin, 1976).

Bandamanna Saga

Trans. Hermann Pálsson as *The Confederates* (Edinburgh: Southside Press, 1975).

Trans. W. Bryant Bachman, Jr. in *Four Old Icelandic Sagas and Other Tales* (Lanham, Md.: University Press of America, 1985), which also includes a translation of *Gunnlaug Serpent-Tongue's Saga*.

"Ale-Hood"

Included in *Hrafnkel's Saga and Other Stories*, trans. Hermann Pálsson (London: Penguin Books, 1971).

Eyrbyggja Saga

Trans. William Morris and Eirik Magnusson (London: Longmans, Green, 1892).

Trans. Paul Schach and Lee M. Hollander (Lincoln, Neb.: University of Nebraska Press, 1959).

Trans. Hermann Pálsson and Paul Edwards (London: Penguin Books, revised ed., 1989).

Chronologies

All dates are approximate for events of the ninth through eleventh centuries on which the sagas were based.

Njal's Saga

930.	Njal born.
940.	Hallgerd born.
945.	Gunnar born.
975.	Gunnar marries Hallgerd.
990.	Gunnar killed.
1000.	Conversion to Christianity.
1005.	Fifth Court established.
1010.	Hoskuld killed, Njal's house burned.
1014.	Battle of Clontarf for throne of Ireland.
1015.	Reconciliation of Kari and Flosi.

Grettir's Saga

997.	Grettir born.
1022.	Grettir outlawed.
1042.	Grettir killed.

Laxdaela Saga

870-930.	Settlement of Iceland.
915.	Arrival of Unn in Iceland.
938.	Birth of Olaf the Peacock.
963.	Birth of Snorri.
970.	Birth of Kjartan and Bolli.
973.	Birth of Gudrun.
998.	Kjartan and Bolli go to Norway.
1003.	Kjartan killed.
1006.	Bolli killed.
1031.	Snorri dies.
1060.	Gudrun dies.

Egil's Saga

890.	Grim arrives in Iceland.
900.	Thorolf born.
910.	Egil born.
915-925.	Thorolf abroad.
927.	Egil's first journey abroad.
937.	Battle for Athelstan's throne; Thorolf killed.
945.	Egil's second journey abroad.
949.	Egil's third journey abroad.
955.	Egil's final journey abroad.
957.	Egil settles permanently in Iceland.
990.	Egil dies.

The action of *Bandamanna Saga* probably belongs to the late tenth century as Christianity is not mentioned and the Althing is well developed. ''Ale-Hood'' dates from Snorri's priesthood, early eleventh century. The major action of *Eyrbyggja Saga* occurs between 986, the year Eirik the Red was outlawed and moved to Greenland, and 1008, when Styr, Snorri's father-in-law, was killed.

Kings of Norway

Harald I Fair-Hair	870-930
Eirik Blood-Axe	930-934
Hakon I the Good	934-961
Harald II Greypate	961-970
Earl Hakon of Lade	970-995
Olaf I Tryggvason	995-1000
Earls Eirik and Sven	1000-1016
St. Olaf II	1016-1030

Adapted from: Karen Larsen, *A History of Norway* (Princeton: Princeton University Press, 1948), p. 569.

1. Title page of *Landnámabók*, the first saga printed in Iceland, 1688. Piety and justice are emphasized as the fruits of monarchical rule. Viking ships above the title are depicted sailing toward Thule (Iceland) in preparation for settlement c. 870.

Credit: Fiske Icelandic Collection, Kroch Library, Cornell University, Ithaca, New York.

2. Ingólfur Arnarson, legendary founder of Iceland, from 1688 printed edition of *Landnámabók.* The Icelandic hero is here depicted much as an ancient Roman soldier would in Baroque art — that is, much as a Renaissance soldier. Here, Ingólfur the founder, depicted on the frontispiece of Iceland's record of settlement and ownership, symbolically surveys the fruit of his labors.

Credit: Fiske Icelandic Collection, Kroch Library, Cornell University, Ithaca, New York.

« Veux-tu accepter ce cadeau ? » demanda Nial.

3. Nineteenth-century depiction of Njal, his wife Bergthora, and foster-son Hoskuld, with his sons sourly looking on, from Jules Gourdault's translation of *Njal's Saga*, *Gunnar et Nial* (Tours: A. Mame, 1886). The saga's characters appear much like the Wagnerian heroes then popular in Europe.

Credit: Fiske Icelandic Collection, Kroch Library, Cornell University, Ithaca, New York.

« Souviens-toi du soufflet que tu me donnas! »

4. Hallgerd reminds Gunnar that he slapped her and refuses to lend him some of her hair to repair his bowstring. Gunnar's mother Rannveig looks on. Gunnar is then slain. From Gourdault's translation of *Njal's Saga*, 1886.

Credit: Fiske Icelandic Collection, Kroch Library, Cornell University, Ithaca, New York.

Thjostolf came up to her

5. Thjostolf speaks with Hallgerd as depicted in the Helgafell illustrated edition of the Magnus Magnusson-Hermann Pálsson translation of *Njal's Saga* (Reykjavik: Helgafell, 1968). Sketch by Gunnlaugur Scheving is a twentieth-century realization of the characters.

Credit: Fiske Icelandic Collection, Kroch Library, Cornell University, Ithaca, New York.

He lunged right-handed at Sigurd Lambason

6. Kari slaying Sigurd Lambason. Sketch by Thorvaldur Skulason from the Helgafell edition of the Magnusson-Pálsson translation of *Njal's Saga*. As in the sketch of Thjostolf and Hallgerd, the artist is more concerned with catching the mood of the scene than with literal depiction, as was the case in the nineteenth-century drawings.

Credit: Fiske Icelandic Collection, Kroch Library, Cornell University, Ithaca, New York.

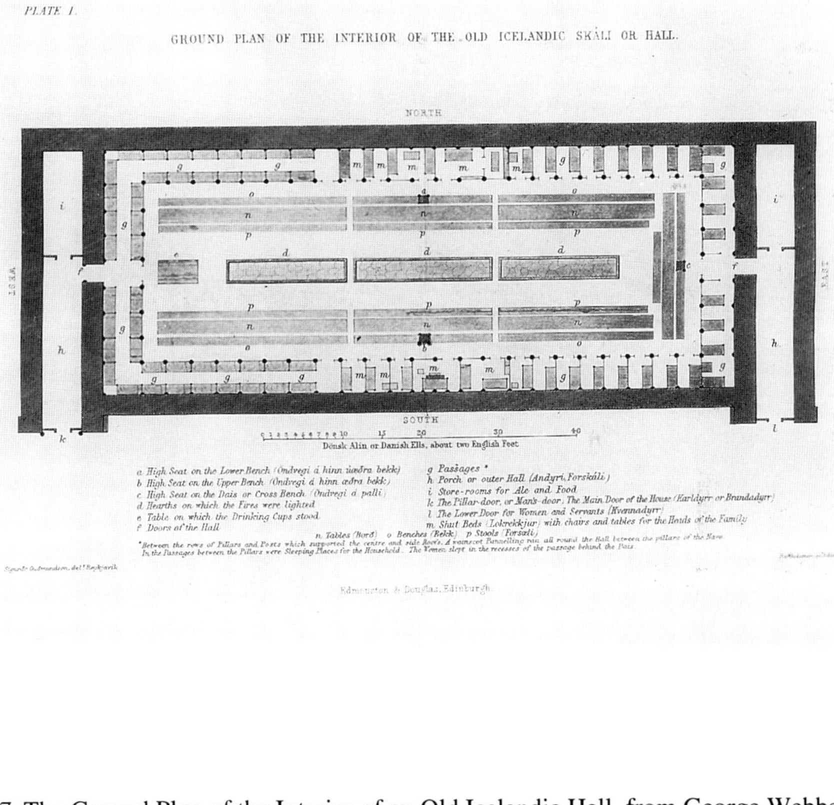

7. The Ground Plan of the Interior of an Old Icelandic Hall, from George Webbe Dasent's translation of *The Story of Burnt Njal* (Edinburgh: Edmonston and Douglas, 1861), volume one. Great chiefs like Njal, Egil, or Snorri would own such a hall and be able to accommodate many followers there. The hall could be turned into a fortress if attacked that was so impregnable only trickery or arson could defeat the defenders.

Credit: Fiske Icelandic Collection, Kroch Library, Cornell University, Ithaca, New York.

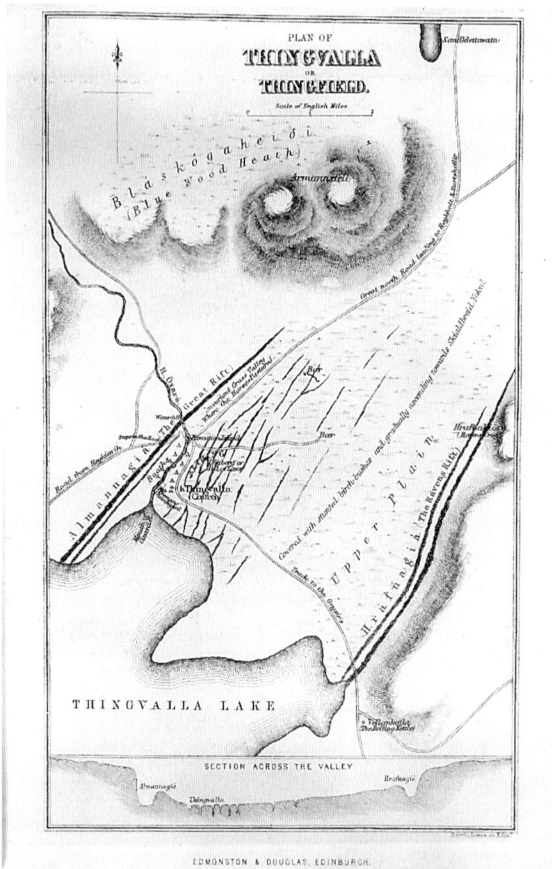

8. Map of Thingvellir (literally, the valley where the Thing met) from Dasent's edition of *Njal's Saga.* The Law Rock is the higher of two places noted amid the dark lines in the center, which depict small inlets of water. A church is the lower of the two places noted in this region. The Almannagjá contains rugged cliffs through whose passes the Thing could be reached. The chiefs set up their booths between here and the Law Rock.

Credit: Fiske Icelandic Collection, Kroch Library, Cornell University, Ithaca, New York.

9. View of Thingvellir from Almannagjá. The Law Rock would be to the left of the church visible in the distance. This is one of the many photographs by Frederick W. W. Howells taken in the 1890s capturing the life and landscape of old Iceland. Much remained unchanged since the days of the sagas.

Credit: Fiske Icelandic Collection, Kroch Library, Cornell University, Ithaca, New York.

10. The pool in which murderesses were drowned at Thingvellir also provides another view of the varied and spectacular landscape in which Icelanders made their laws and settled their legal disputes. Photography by Howells.

Credit: Fiske Icelandic Collection, Kroch Library, Cornell University, Ithaca, New York.

11. In this photograph by Howells, the Law Rock itself, the symbol and center of Iceland's republican government, dominates the scene.

Credit: Fiske Icelandic Collection, Kroch Library, Cornell University, Ithaca, New York.

12. These small ferries, photographed by Howells in the 1890s, still resemble the boats used in the days of the sagas. The barren yet varied and spectacular Icelandic landscape also comes through dramatically in this photo.

Credit: Fiske Icelandic Collection, Kroch Library, Cornell University, Ithaca, New York.

13. The slopes of Mt. Hekla, an active volcano as late as 1845, illustrate the Icelandic soil far better suited for grazing than for agriculture. Note the scarcity of trees in this, or any of the other photographs by Howells in this volume.

Credit: Fiske Icelandic Collection, Kroch Library, Cornell University, Ithaca, New York.

14. Howells photographed these turf houses at Laugarvatn. They resembled the dwellings of humble Icelanders in the days of the sagas, and explain why so few ruins dot the landscape. Timber was scarce, used mostly for great halls and temples (later churches), and turf did not survive the ravages of time.

Credit: Fiske Icelandic Collection, Kroch Library, Cornell University, Ithaca, New York.

15. These Icelandic farmers at Galtalakur, photographed by Howells c. 1900, may have resembled their medieval ancestors. Houses still have turf roofs although they are made of timber with glass windows. Subsistence agriculture persisted in Iceland into the twentieth century.

Credit: Fiske Icelandic Collection, Kroch Library, Cornell University, Ithaca, New York.

16. This church and parsonage at Hruni, glass windows excepted, which Howells photographed c. 1900 resembles the structures built by chiefs with imported timber during Iceland's republican era. Note the simplicity of design and, again, sparse landscape.

Credit: Fiske Icelandic Collection, Kroch Library, Cornell University, Ithaca, New York.

Bibliography

Excludes introductions and other essays which accompany texts listed in *Notes on Translations and Spelling*.

Adair, Douglass. "Experience Must Be Our Only Guide: History, Democratic Theory, and the United States Constitution," in Ray Allen Billington, ed., *The Reinterpretation of Early American History: Essays in Honor of John Edwin Pomfret.* San Marino, Cal.: The Huntington Library, 1966: 129-148.

_____. "That Politics May Be Reduced to a Science: David Hume, James Madison, and the Tenth Federalist," *Huntington Library Quarterly* 20 (1957): 343-360.

Allen, Richard F. *Fire and Iron: Critical Approaches to Njal's Saga.* Pittsburgh: University of Pittsburgh Press, 1971.

Andersson, Theodore M. *The Icelandic Family Saga: An Analytical Reading.* Cambridge, Mass.: Harvard University Press, 1967.

_____. ed. *Scandinavian Studies*, special issue on Icelandic Sagas 60 (1988).

Aquinas, St. Thomas. "The Essence of Law," in Anton C. Pegis, ed., *Introduction to St. Thomas Aquinas.* New York: Random House, 1948.

Austin, John. *The Province of Jurisprudence*, H. L. A. Hart, ed. London: Weidenfeld and Nicolson, 1954; orginally published 1832.

Burke, Edmund. *Reflections on the Revolution in France*, Thomas H. D. Mahoney, ed. New York: Liberal Arts Press, 1955; originally published 1791.

Byock, Jesse. *Feud in the Icelandic Saga.* Berkeley: University of California Press, 1982.

_____. "Governmental Order in Early Medieval Iceland," *Viator* 17 (1986): 19-34.

_____. *Medieval Iceland: Society, Sagas, Power.* Berkeley: University of California Press, 1988.

Clover, Carol J. "The Politics of Scarcity: Notes on the Sex Ratio in Early Scandinavia," *Scandinavian Studies* 60 (1988): 147-188.

_____. "Regardless of Sex: Men, Women, and Power in Northern Europe," *Speculum* 68 (1993): 363-388.

_____. ed. with Lindow, John. *Old Norse-Icelandic Literature: A Critical Guide, Islandica* 45, Ithaca, N.Y.: Cornell University Press, 1985.

Dworkin, Ronald. *Taking Rights Seriously.* Cambridge, Mass.: Harvard University Press, 1977.

Frank, Jerome. *Law and the Modern Mind.* New York: Brentano's, 1930.

Friedman, Lawrence. *The Legal System.* New York: Russell Sage Foundation, 1975.

Fuller, Lon. "American Legal Realism," *University of Pennsylvania Law Review* 82 (1934): 429-461.

Hart, H. L. A. *The Concept Of Law.* Oxford: Oxford University Press, 1961.

Jochens, Jenny. "The Medieval Icelandic Heroine: Fact or Fiction?," *Viator* 17 (1986): 35-50.

Ker, W. P. *The Dark Ages.* New York: Mentor Books, 1958; reprint of 1904 edition.

_____. *Epic and Romance: Essays on Medieval Literature.* New York: Dover, 1957; reprint of 1896 edition.

Kevelson, Roberta. *The Law as a System of Signs.* New York: Plenum Press, 1988.

Lewis, C. S. *The Abolition of Man.* New York: Macmillan, 1943.

Lincoln, Abraham. *Collected Works*, Roy P. Basler, ed. Volume One. New Brunswick, N.J.: Rutgers University Press, 1953.

Lönnroth, Lars. *Njal's Saga: A Critical Introduction.* Berkeley: Unviersity of California Press, 1976.

Mill, John Stuart. *Utilitarianism.* London: J. M. Dent, 1910; originally published 1862.

Miller, William Ian. *Bloodtaking and Peacemaking: Feud, Law, and Society in Saga Iceland.* Chicago: University of Chicago Press, 1990.

Murphy, Jeffrie, and Coleman, Jules. *The Philosophy of Law: An Introduction to Jurisprudence.* Totowa, N.J.: Rowman & Allenheld, 1984.

Pocock, J. G. A. *The Machiavellian Moment: Florentine Political Thought and the Atlantic Republican Tradition.* Princeton: Princeton University Press, 1975.

Rahe, Paul. *Republics: Ancient and Modern Classical Republicanism and the American Revolution.* Chapel Hill, N.C.: University of North Carolina Press, 1992.

Schach, Paul. *Icelandic Sagas.* Boston: Twayne Publishers, 1984.

Scott, Sir Walter. ''Abstract of the *Eyrbyggia-Saga*,'' in Henry Weber and Robert Jamieson, eds., *Illustrations of Northern Antiquities.* London and Edinburgh, 1814, pp. 475-513.

Sveinsson, Einar. *Njal's Saga: A Literary Masterpiece*, trans. Paul Schach. Lincoln: University of Nebraska Press, 1971.

About the Author

William Pencak was born in 1951 in Brooklyn, New York. He was graduated *magna cum laude* in 1972 from Columbia University in New York City, where he also received a Ph.D. in American History in 1978. He has taught at the Stevens Institute of Technology, Columbia University, Tufts University, the University of California at San Diego, California State University, Chico, and the University of Monterrey, Mexico, where he was Fulbright Professor of International Studies in 1988-1989. He is currently Professor of History at the Pennsylvania State University. He previously held an Andrew Mellon Fellowship at Duke University and a National Endowment for the Humanities Fellowship at the Shelby Cullom Davis Center for Historical Studies, Princeton University. He has also received grants from the American Philosophical Society and the Huntington Library in Pasadena, California. Pencak has previously authored four books — *War, Politics, & Revolution in Provincial Massachusetts* (1981), *America's Burke: The Mind of Thomas Hutchinson* (1982), *For God and Country: The American Legion, 1919-1941* (1989), and *History, Signing In: Studies in History and Semiotics* (1993) — and co-edited six books: a five-volume series based on conferences he organized for the New-York Historical Society from 1983 to 1987 (published 1988-1992) and, with Frank Freidel, *The White House: The First Two Hundred Years* (1994). He organized the first session on Semiotics and History for the American Historical Association's Annual Meeting in 1987, and served as the first historian on the Executive Board of the Semiotics Society of America from 1991 to 1993. In 1991 he co-edited, with Brooke Williams, a special issue of *Semiotica* on *Semiotics and History.* He currently edits *Pennsylvania History* and is completing a biography of William Penn, to be published by Northeastern University Press.

INDEX OF PRINCIPAL CHARACTERS

2. *Njal's Saga*

3. *Grettir's Saga*

4. *Laxdaela Saga*

5. *Egil's Saga*

6. *Bandamanna Saga*

INDEX OF PLACES, SUBJECTS, AND NON-SAGA PEOPLE

VALUE INQUIRY BOOK SERIES

VIBS

1. Noel Balzer, **The Human Being as a Logical Thinker.**

2. Archie J. Bahm, **Axiology: The Science of Values.**

3. H. P. P. (Hennie) Lötter, **Justice for an Unjust Society.**

4. H. G. Callaway, **Context for Meaning and Analysis: A Critical Study in the Philosophy of Language.**

5. Benjamin S. Llamzon, **A Humane Case for Moral Intuition.**

6. James R. Watson, **Between Auschwitz and Tradition: Postmodern Reflections on the Task of Thinking.** A volume in **Holocaust and Genocide Studies.**

7. Robert S. Hartman, **Freedom to Live: The Robert Hartman Story,** edited by Arthur R. Ellis. A volume in **Hartman Institute Axiology Studies.**

8. Archie J. Bahm, **Ethics: The Science of Oughtness.**

9. George David Miller: **An Idiosyncratic Ethics; Or, the Lauramachean Ethics.**

10. Joseph P. DeMarco, **A Coherence Theory in Ethics.**

11. Frank G. Forrest, **Valuemetrics$^{\aleph}$: The Science of Personal and Professional Ethics.** A volume in **Hartman Institute Axiology Studies.**

12. William Gerber, **The Meaning of Life: Insights of the World's Great Thinkers.**

13. Richard T. Hull, Editor, **A Quarter Century of Value Inquiry: Presidential Addresses of the American Society for Value Inquiry.** A volume in **Histories and Addresses of Philosophical Societies.**

14. William Gerber, **Nuggets of Wisdom from Great Jewish Thinkers: From Biblical Times to the Present.**

15. Sidney Axinn, **The Logic of Hope: Extensions of Kant's View of Religion.**

16. Messay Kebede, **Meaning and Development.**

17. Amihud Gilead, **The Platonic Odyssey: A Philosophical-Literary Inquiry into the *Phaedo.***

18. Necip Fikri Alican, **Mill's Principle of Utility: A Defense of John Stuart Mill's Notorious Proof.** A volume in **Universal Justice.**

19. Michael H. Mitias, Editor, **Philosophy and Architecture.**

20. Roger T. Simonds, **Rational Individualism: The Perennial Philosophy of Legal Interpretation.** A volume in **Natural Law Studies.**

21. William Pencak, **The Conflict of Law and Justice in the Icelandic Sagas.**